Breaking Free... From Me
Getting Self in Sync with the Big Picture

J. Matthew Nance

Copyright © 2012 by J. Matthew Nance.

All rights reserved. No part of this book may be used or reproduced by any means, graphic, electronic, or mechanical, including photocopying, recording, taping or by any information storage retrieval system without the written permission of the publisher except in the case of brief quotations embodied in critical articles and reviews.

ISBN: 978-1-4497-4882-1 (e)
ISBN: 978-1-4497-4883-8 (sc)
ISBN: 978-1-4497-4884-5 (hc)

Library of Congress Control Number: 2012907169

WestBow Press books may be ordered through booksellers or by contacting:

WestBow Press
A Division of Thomas Nelson
1663 Liberty Drive
Bloomington, IN 47403
www.westbowpress.com
1-(866) 928-1240

Because of the dynamic nature of the Internet, any web addresses or links contained in this book may have changed since publication and may no longer be valid. The views expressed in this work are solely those of the author and do not necessarily reflect the views of the publisher, and the publisher hereby disclaims any responsibility for them.

Any people depicted in stock imagery provided by Thinkstock are models, and such images are being used for illustrative purposes only.

Certain stock imagery © Thinkstock.

Printed in the United States of America

WestBow Press rev. date: 05/21/2012

To Cheryl

*Apart from new life in Christ,
your love is the greatest gift I have ever received.*

*You are beautiful, my darling,
Beautiful beyond words.
You have captured my heart, my treasure, my bride.
You hold it hostage with one glance of your eyes.
Song of Solomon 4:1,9*

Contents

Foreword vii
It's Not Easy Being Me! 1
Am I Smarter than Jonah? 7
The World Revolves Around Me! 18
One Whale of a Jail! 31
Failure Is Not Final! 44
Is There Hope for America? 54
Welcome to My Pity Party! 68
When Serving God Brings Out the Very Worst in Me 84
Developing a Heart for My City 94
Where Is God When I Am Self-Absorbed? 105
When the Church Becomes Self-Absorbed 116
So Long Self! 128
Appendix A 142
Appendix B 143
Endnotes 145

Foreword
By Jerry Rankin

MATTHEW NANCE HAS BOTH A rare gift of insight into spiritual truths as well as the ability to communicate those insights in a convicting way. *"Breaking Free...From Me"* exposes the compelling need for you and me to be aligned with God in order for life to become what it was intended to be.

Skillfully identifying Old Testament Jonah's problem as one of self-absorption, Nance paints a picture of each of us when we become entrapped in disappointment and bitterness because God is not following our agenda. We usually realize, at least in theory, the futility of trying to run from God. However *"Breaking Free...From Me"* challenges our unrecognized tendency toward self-directed living, and shows that tendency to be the same as Jonah fleeing to Tarshish instead of obeying God.

If you are familiar with the Old story of Jonah, you may think of it simply as a favorite children's story. Most adults do not find the exploits of Jonah and repentance of an ancient city relevant to life today. However, as you will discover while reading *"Breaking Free...From Me,"* the Jonah story is much more relevant than we would have dared to believe.

If you are like most everyone on this planet, you may think the world revolves around self. Though self-absorbed living may not cause you to end up in the belly of a whale, you may find yourself living in a dungeon of self-will, self-indulgence, self-righteousness and self-interest, robbing you of the freedom and life of victory God intends for you. You and I usually don't cope with life's storms any better than Jonah, often leaving us feeling hopeless about the future. However, *"Breaking Free...From Me"* will inspire you to discover the God who gives us second chances to live beyond self.

The chapter on *"An Ego Addict's 12 Steps to Prison Break"* is a highlight worth the price of the book. These 12 steps provide deliverance from the dilemma of self-centered, self-sufficient living. If you are overwhelmed by crisis and failure, here you will discover a "get out of jail free card!"

Nance does not neglect the missionary message as he challenges you to develop a heart for the city, both the city where you live as well as the world's urban centers. Like Nineveh, our world is lost and desperately needs people who will proclaim the possibility of averting the judgment of God through the acceptance of His love. One of the most powerful chapters is focused on painting the church as the Jonah of today--asleep in the storm, self-absorbed, pre-occupied with comfort and prejudiced toward people who are different.

Pastors, missionaries and Christian workers will readily identify with Nance's sensitivity and vulnerability in his chapter, *"When Serving God Brings out the Worst in Me."* A position of leadership often blinds us to reality and subtly diverts us from dependence on God. Pride is the fruit of being self-absorbed and invariably leads to disappointment when God chooses not to fulfill our expectations.

"Breaking Free...From Me" is not another of the prolific number of "self-help" books being published today. In these pages, you will find refreshing, in-depth Bible study with relevant application. The narrative of Jonah will gain a new relevance as you respond to personal revelations and apply the truths and insights of this book to your life.

It's Not Easy Being Me!

RECENTLY, I WENT OVER TO my friend Ron's house for an evening with a small group of friends. As I walked through the front door, a playful puppy came bounding in through the back door. Jack, the puppy, was remarkably well mannered for being only four months old. Although he seemed eager to jump up and lick my face, he sat obediently on the floor, just as he had been trained to do.

When other friends arrived, they too noticed how well-behaved Jack was. As we finished our coffee cake, we all sat down and put our dishes on the coffee table at Jack's level. The temptation was too great for Jack. Suddenly, in one big gulp, Jack scarfed down someone's piece of cake, and then stuck his muzzle down into someone else's coffee and inhaled it! Everyone's opinion of Jack instantly changed. He was no longer the obedient puppy we thought he was.

I must admit that I am often just like Jack. One minute I seem thrilled to obey my Master and humbly do as He says. The next minute I act like I have no master but me. It's not easy being me!

One of life's greatest challenges is learning to deal with "self" appropriately. What do I do with me? Why do I sometimes feel like the more I live by the "what's best for me" principle, the more I feel that life is meaningless?

Some have reacted to self-absorption by going to the extreme of thinking of self as a worm. There is an old hymn that says Jesus died for "such a worm as I." Though in the Bible a few people call themselves worms, God never calls man a worm. He created us in His image. If we are to have emotional stability, we must know and deeply feel that we are indeed of great value to our Creator. We are of infinite value to Him.[1] Repeat this statement out loud five times:

I am of great value to my Creator.

Our typical problem today is not the underrating of self, but the overrating of self. It's the absorption in all things relating to ourselves that messes us up. Every generation has a title pinned to it in history books.

In the 1960s, we had the Baby Boomer generation. Today's young people are sometimes known as the "Me Generation." This generation says that the goal of life is to satisfy self. God can help *me* reach *my* goal. He is my "divine bellboy, a cosmic waiter, or heavenly room service."[2]

In this generation, self has become the American idol. We live in the generation of self:

- self-indulgence
- self-will
- self-service
- self-gratification
- self-righteousness
- self-sufficiency
- self-interest

Absorption with self affects us negatively. Self-absorption as a means to fulfillment brings only disillusion. Maybe you are looking for an alternative to popular culture's "me-first" approach to life. This book is for you.

If you are frustrated by a pointless pursuit of "the good life," read on. Tired of a culture that says *you* are all that matters? Desperate for a life that truly satisfies? Then you simply must keep reading.

Am I not to be most concerned about myself and how everything affects me? What's the big deal about living for self? Well, let's see. A focus on self leads to a distrust of others. I start to think, *Is there anyone that I can really be honest with? Should I risk telling someone that I am both good and bad, caring yet cruel, selfless and selfish, a brave warrior yet a frightened child? Dare I let someone in on the secrets of my life? Where does God come into play in my search for self?*

Jonah is the patron saint of self-absorption. From the belly of a whale, he finds out the consequences of self-obsession. If there is one phrase spoken by Jonah as a summary of his life, it is the phrase uttered at the climax of his tug-of-war with God: "It is better for me ..." There you have it. In all things, Jonah's primary concern is *self*.

Ready for some tough introspection?

- Do you find yourself doing enjoyable things excessively while avoiding unpleasant things?
- Do you use the greater amount of your energy on personal vanity?

- Are hidden motives often driving your actions?
- Are you hypersensitive toward criticism?
- Do you tend to be egocentric and pleasure-driven?
- Would others describe you as more competitive than cooperative?

If these questions hit close to home, then read on. We will discover in this book the remedy to the above predicaments.

A life lived for self cannot satisfy. For example, some people have achieved success, fame, and wealth only to discover it is not enough. The expected satisfaction was not there. Instead, they became more self-centered and miserable.

Jonah knows all about being self-centered and miserable. The Jonah story is full of emotional drama. While people today often put up a facade and follow the unwritten rule that negative emotions are not to be admitted before God and others, Jonah bursts on the scene like a five-year-old spilling out his inner feelings before God and everybody. How refreshing!

Jonah is narrow-minded, aggressively disobedient, lacking in compassion, and all wrapped up in himself. Is there anything good to be said about Jonah? Certainly! Jonah is brave enough to be utterly honest before God about his own feelings and perspective. His is the story of the transparent, down-to-earth confessions of a struggling human.

Plot Jonah's spiritual progress on a graph, and the resulting picture looks like a roller coaster ride. At times, he is very down and very far from God, then he swings back up and is very excited about obeying God—only to go back down again into depression followed yet again by another misguided upswing.

What a struggle Jonah has getting self in sync with the big picture of life. I want to shake Jonah and say to him, "Jonah! Wake up to reality! You act as if life is a role-playing game in which *you* are the producer-director-god, and the Creator becomes your puppet. The little skit you are producing is one huge tragedy. Jonah, that lifestyle just doesn't work. It's no fun at all!"

Yet when I look at Jonah, I find I am looking in a mirror. I am Jonah. Sometimes it's not at all easy being me. It's enough to make me want to run away from home. That's how Jonah handles it.

I would like to think of my own journey as one of steady growth, but that would just be my Sunday-morning facade. In reality, there have been upswings in my life when the sense of God's presence has been profound and overwhelming, as well as times when my old self-centered nature causes serious downswings.

In these downswings, I try reasoning with myself. *I should not have hurtful feelings toward other people. I know I should not feel that I am better than others. I consider myself a Christian, and these feelings are all wrong. So I must not admit them to anyone. I certainly must not let God in on my feelings.* This is only an attempt to sweep the elephant in the room under the rug. When I ignore my negative emotions, my feeling of hopelessness grows bigger. When I am bold enough to admit that I am struggling, I take the first step. Being honest about myself before God and others brings refreshing change into my life.

Jonah reminds us how difficult it is to balance our desire to control our own destiny with the reality that Someone Else is really in charge here. The Jonah drama teaches us so much. Even young children can find an everyday application of the Jonah story.

Elementary students tend to get frightened when they hear about the ocean and all the scary fish that live in it. A teacher tried to reassure her class, as many attempt to do, about the safety of the ocean.

"I don't want you to be afraid of going into seawater. There are no sea creatures that can swallow you whole," the teacher said.

A little girl raised her hand. "At church they said a great fish swallowed Jonah whole," she said.

The teacher laughed. "That's impossible. It could never happen."

"When I get to heaven, I'll ask Jonah myself," the girl said.

"What If Jonah didn't make it to heaven?" the teacher replied.

"Then *you* can ask him!"

As we visualize all that happens to Jonah, we can't help but laugh. God uses humor to get His point across and relieve tension, as does this elementary girl's story.

In order to break free from me, I sometimes need someone to come along and say, "Snap out of it already!" Pastor Skip Heitzig of New Mexico had to do just that. Skip went to visit a lockdown ward in a local hospital. He spoke with a girl there who was depressed and even suicidal. He spoke kindly but firmly to her, saying, "You know, it's not all about you. God has work for you to do. His plan for you isn't over yet. There are other people who need you." She was astonished. She had not been thinking about others at all. Two weeks later, she approached him at church and thanked him for the gentle jolt back to reality. She was lifted out of darkness by realizing life had a greater purpose than herself, and she became determined to find out God's purpose for her life.³

If you want to find meaning in life, you must look beyond your own existence.

True, *sustained* self-worth only comes when you have a genuine relationship with the loving heavenly Father, trusting Him enough to surrender who you are to Him. Right now, come before God powerless and broken. Give yourself fully to Him. By trusting in His love and care for you, life becomes what He intends it to be. "Behold the splendor of a human heart which trusts that it is loved!"⁴

How will this book help you? If you are desperate for a different kind of life that really satisfies, then you will find in these pages the way to get self in sync with the bigger picture of life. Through applying the principles found in this book, you will

- discover the remedy for self-absorption,
- pinpoint mental roadblocks keeping you from the joy of truly giving self away,
- discover God's desire to use you in making a difference in your city,
- learn how to view yourself through God's eyes, and
- move on from "Me-ville" to places you never dared visit.

Inward searching has some value, but in reality, it can easily become merely another form of self-absorption. It can cause you to get stuck in navel-gazing mode. Sometimes there is terrible paralysis in self-analysis. Though this book requires much introspection, don't linger long while you are reading it. A brisk read-through of this book is best, followed by a long, meaningful life of self-less living. Learn to look away from self.

Jonah learns about looking away from self the hard way, as did author Rudyard Kipling's character Harvey in his classic novel *Captains Courageous*.⁵ Fifteen-year-old Harvey is the son of a wealthy railroad tycoon. While on a transatlantic steamship, Harvey is washed overboard and rescued by fishermen. For the first time in his spoiled existence, Harvey is cold, wet, and forgotten. He tries to convince the fishermen of his parents' great wealth, but Harvey's pleas to be taken to shore, despite the promise of a generous reward from his father, are ignored. Harvey is forced to clean the guts out of fish to earn his keep.

Harvey cannot believe his terrible circumstances. He is disgusted and overwhelmed by the backbreaking work, the long hours, the stench of fish guts, and the cold, wet weather. But over time, Harvey's mind and body toughen. He learns to work with his hands and weather the trials of the open sea. Slowly, Harvey begins to enjoy his new life. He admires the strength and intelligence of his new companions.

When they finally reach land, Harvey wires his parents. After rushing to arrive at the port, his parents are amazed to find a transformed son. The Harvey they knew was a lazy, demanding mama's boy. Here they found an industrious, serious, and considerate young man who was ready to start a successful career in his father's shipping lines.

Harvey found that there was more to life than self. Have you discovered that for yourself? How can you get self in sync with life's bigger picture?

David Zimmerman has written a timely book[6] for the Me Generation in which he reminds us that when we create a contemporary holy trinity of me, myself, and I, we pretend that we live in a world existing just for us called Me-ville. It's time that we pray the title of his book: "Lord, Deliver Us from Me-ville."

Is there anything more to life than merely me? The encouraging answer is an emphatic yes! As you read, you will begin to look at life from a different angle. A new plan for your life will unfold. At first, it may all feel a bit awkward. However, as self gets in sync with the bigger picture, life will become all it was meant to be.

Am I Smarter than Jonah?

Are you smarter than a fifth grader? Many people would like to think they are. The television show *Are You Smarter than a Fifth Grader?* pits a class of fifth-grade students against an adult guest. The adult is asked questions from first- to fifth-grade levels. Inevitably the fifth-graders end up winning the show, and the adult must on national television admit that he or she is indeed not smarter than a fifth-grader.

We often overrate our own intelligence. The truth is, we seldom understand what constitutes true intellect. It's possible to have a head full of facts but have no clue what to do in a given situation. To be truly smart is to receive God's help in applying the knowledge you have to the situation at hand.

Jonah considers himself to be pretty smart. He believes he is more intelligent than the designer of the universe. He knows better than God! After all, God seems so remote, so disconnected, and so seemingly unconcerned about what is best for Jonah, who is live on the scene with, he believes, the best intel!

Are you smarter than Jonah? Find out by answering this four-question test. If you answer all four questions correctly, you will have proven that you are, in fact, smarter than Jonah. It's that simple. Sorry to say, there's no million-dollar prize.

Answering the questions correctly involves more than just verbally giving the correct answer. It means letting God change you into someone who doesn't think or act like Jonah. Ultimately, whether or not you are smarter than Jonah depends on how well you cultivate a heart of obedience to God. That kind of heart is worth way more than a million dollars.

Ready for the first question? Here we go.

Question #1:
What is the most common reason some people who are called to missions don't go?

- Some people do not have the funds needed to quit their jobs and move overseas.

- Parents do not approve of their married children taking the grandkids away to Timbuktu.
- Fear of the unknown is an understandable reason for not going.
- Some people fail to meet the stiff qualifications for appointment by a mission-sending organization.
- The sacrifice required is too great. One man feeling almost called to mission work overseas said, "If I go over there, who will feed my dog, Fuzzy Wuzzy?"

There are so many reasons people say no to God's call to missions. What is the greatest reason? Let's ask Jonah.

> The Lord gave this message to Jonah son of Amittai: "Get up and go to the great city of Nineveh! Announce my judgment against it because I have seen how wicked its people are.
> But Jonah got up and went in the opposite direction in order to get away from the Lord. He went down to the seacoast, to the port of Joppa, where he found a ship leaving for Tarshish. He bought a ticket and went on board, hoping that by going away to the west he could escape from the Lord. (Jonah 1:1–3)

God says go, Jonah says no. Jonah's reason for saying no to God remains the primary reason people say no to Him today: *self-absorption*.

Jonah hears God's voice clearly. There is no pretending that he doesn't hear the phone ring. Jonah picks up the phone, hears the command of the Lord, and hangs up on God. Instead of saying, "Yes, sir!" he slams the phone down and says, "No way!"

During our years in East Asia, my wife Cheryl and I met a missionary kid named Tessa. She shared with me a time when she slammed the phone down and said no to her parents, who were trying to guide her. Tessa said, "Conceit and self-absorption used to be close friends of mine in middle school. They were such good friends that it drove a wedge between my parents and me. Those friends still show up unannounced sometimes."

Jonah is so immersed in himself that it leads him to hang up on the God of the universe. He refuses to go to another land and lead the people there to turn back to God. Sure, Jonah feels guilty about ignoring God's call. Before the call, he was relaxed and in a place of rest. Now he is a ball of nervous energy. He's thinking, *What will God do when He finds out I refuse to go where He said? Where can I run and hide?*

To make sure God doesn't come around and help him pack his missionary bags, Jonah tries the impossible: running from God. Come on, Jonah! Think about it. How fast do you have to run to outrun God? How far would you have to run to get to a place where God *isn't*?

What is going on in Jonah's mind? Why doesn't he simply obey? Maybe he is just one of those people who hangs an emotional "Do Not Disturb" sign on the door to his heart. "God, I don't want to be troubled by your agenda for me. Life is all about doing my own thing."

Maybe Jonah doesn't feel God is being fair by inconveniencing him with such a request. After all, Jonah's hammock is waiting in the backyard.

Maybe he doesn't like the particular race of "inferior" and unbelievably cruel people who live where God wants Jonah to go. They are just not worth the sacrifice required to get there or the danger in being there.

Whatever the "maybe" may be, Jonah is simply too wrapped up in his own life agenda to be concerned with God's agenda. Are you smarter than Jonah?

Margaret wasn't. Margaret knew she and her husband were supposed to be missionaries. She and her husband both felt clearly the call of God to leave their current life behind, move to a needy country, learn the language, and love the people into the Kingdom of God. However, her fear of what would happen to their children if they lived among the barbaric heathens consumed her. The education their children were receiving at their private Christian school was top-notch, sheltering them adequately from the evils of the world. She really liked her kitchen, too, and she knew she couldn't take it with her. She was a bit relieved that they were in so much debt that it would be impossible to leave anyway.

Ask yourself these questions:

- If God were to call me to serve Him on the mission field, what things would make it difficult to go?
- Even despite those things, if He calls me, would I be willing to go?

Self-absorption responds to God's call by thinking of all the things that would have to be sacrificed. A man may say, "I would have to give up my dog and my hunting." A woman might say, "I would have to give up my dining room table and my dishes." Self-absorption blinds you from seeing all the things gained if you respond positively to God's call.

In the last two decades of serving the Lord overseas, Cheryl and I have certainly made many unexpected sacrifices. Shortly after arriving in Korea in 1990, my grandmother died, and I was not able to turn around and go back to her funeral. We often felt disconnected from those we love.

There have been car accidents, surgeries, vehicle thefts, betrayal by coworkers, a security crisis—the list goes on. However, we have gained so much more than we have lost. Obeying God by going where He sent us has given us an international perspective on life, an exceptionally strong family, a great love for the diverse peoples of the world, joy in seeing people believe in the Lord and lead their own new churches, and a more vibrant personal relationship of dependency on the Lord. The things gained far outweigh the things given up.

Tessa's family also knows the gains found in obedience. She can relate to being miles away from her family. She says, "While most of my college friends could go home on weekends, home for me is a thousand-dollar plane ticket. My immediate family is in three different countries pursuing the direction God has given us. I would never trade what I have gained for the comfort of having my parents and brother all in one country."

Don't give in to the self-absorption that keeps many people from joyfully serving the Lord on the mission field. True joy comes through obedience, even if it means relocating to an area requiring great sacrifice. Obedience is a form of worship. Overcome self-absorption by letting your ears be sensitive to God's voice. When He says go, will you say no? Or are you smarter than Jonah?

Question #2:
What is the greatest reason for people experiencing stormy, troubled lives?

The book of Jonah is almost like God showing us a comical movie that drives home a very serious point. Visualize a hypothetical Jonah movie: Jonah is enjoying a snooze in the sun on his hammock. He obviously likes living at a relaxed pace. Bring on the coconut juice and suntan oil!

Jonah's lanky body is kicked back on the hammock. He is not exactly a robust bodybuilder. Wimpy and awkward, Jonah is full of talk and full of self. Just think of Barney Fife from *The Andy Griffith Show*, and the picture is clear.

Suddenly, a commanding voice says, "Get up Jonah. Go east to Nineveh, a proud heathen metropolis, exceptionally fortified by high, secure walls and intimidating warriors. Tell them to repent or die."

Lazy Jonah responds to God's call with a jolt of energy, but it's not energy spent obeying. Instead, with his wobbly, unexercised legs, he's running west to the harbor, not east. After boarding a ship, Jonah descends into the vessel's belly and falls into deep sleep. The moment he refuses to relocate to God's destination is the instant Jonah's storm begins.

> But as the ship was sailing along, suddenly the Lord flung a powerful wind over the sea, causing a violent storm that threatened to send them to the bottom… And all this time Jonah was sound asleep down in the hold. (Jonah 1:4–5)

When we ignore God's call to serve Him because we think it will bring trouble, bigger trouble comes into our lives! When we run from the imagined difficulty that comes from following God, the very thing we run into is very real difficulty!

There are many reasons that people experience storms in life. Not all messes are self-made. Sometimes friends and relatives bring their uninvited troubles into our lives. Other times it's the economy or the boss. We live in an imperfect, unpredictable, and sometimes troubling world. However, perhaps the greatest reason our lives may become difficult is our own self-absorption.

In Jonah's case, it was obvious. The storm at sea is his fault. God's agenda is not to Jonah's liking, so he takes off running from God and jumps on a ship where he can hide. His disobedience brings trouble for himself and everyone else on board. Running from God brings a storm at heart and a storm on the sea of life.

Obedience is an issue of authority. God does not have to give us an explanation for His commands. In Jonah's case, God's explanation for sending Jonah to Nineveh is salvation for the people. Jonah is so self-centered that he is willing to let thousands of people die without hearing the name of the Lord.

There in the belly of that vessel, Jonah takes pride in successfully hiding from God. He convinces himself that he is saved from the trouble of following God's call. Satisfied with his prowess at playing hide-and-go-seek with God, Jonah once again returns to his natural habit of laziness. He sings himself a lullaby as the ship rocks him to sleep.

We look at the "Jonah movie" and laugh at his obviously foolish behavior. However, our own disobedience is something that's much more difficult for us to see. We point the finger at Jonah, while the rest of our fingers point back to our own self-centeredness.

Are you smarter than Jonah?

Danny wasn't.

Danny worked hard to become the manager of a professional baseball team. He knew that God was clearly calling him to be a Christian witness among professional athletes. However, Danny ran from that call and ran toward seemingly more desirable goals. There were head-spinning parties with beautiful young females who greatly admired athletes and their managers. There were also lucrative deals to be made.

The glitter and fame gave Danny a real buzz. However, Danny found it embarrassing to tell anyone that he was a follower of Jesus. His passion for worshipping and serving the Lord was gone.

Danny was falling apart on the inside. Life had become all about mood-enhancing women and substances. The self-destruction came into Danny's life so gradually that he didn't really even notice. That's how it is with sin.

We don't like to admit we have created a stormy life. A storm in *my* life? What storm? If we don't see the storm, we might be in the eye of it. The eye of a hurricane is eerily still. While it is seemingly quiet, we are surrounded by hurricane-force winds. When it passes, it certainly isn't quiet or still.

Instead of admitting we have produced a storm, we would rather sleep in the hull of the ship. We would deaden the pain of reality by

- taking happy pills,
- keeping ourselves constantly entertained,
- escaping into our own little private world,
- gorging our way to blissful misery,
- drinking our troubles away,
- working hard in church to avoid God's call, or
- sucking on any anesthesia that promises to pacify.

What may be the greatest reason for personal misery today? The answer to question two is *self-absorption*. Catching on yet? Ask yourself, has my focus on self caused recent difficulties in my life? How so?

Question #3:
What is it that God most often has to deliver us from?

In the next clip, the Jonah movie cuts to the captain confronting Jonah. The captain says, "Jonah! How can you sleep through this terrible storm? Get up and help us throw everything overboard!" Jonah rubs the sleep from his eyes and groggily says, "No need to do that. This storm is my fault. I'm running from God. Just throw me overboard instead."

> Then the sailors picked Jonah up and threw him into the raging sea, and the storm stopped at once! (Jonah 1:15)

We see Jonah flying through the air and splashing into the turbulent sea. For sure, that's the end of old Jonah. Got what he deserved. Bye-bye, Jonah! Then, suddenly, something incredible happens.

> Now the Lord had arranged a great fish to swallow Jonah. And Jonah was inside the fish for three days and three nights. (Jonah 1:17)

Jonah's life is saved! Despite Jonah's readiness for his life to end, God keeps Jonah from drowning. Being self-consumed leads us to ruin our lives and the lives of others. However, God is not content to leave us alone to self-destruct. He seeks to rescue us from self.

What if God had not provided for a big fish to be at just the right place, at just the right time, with his mouth open? Jonah would have drowned. However, Jonah doesn't even care. He has already resigned himself to fate.

One thing about God: He is not fatalistic. He has a plan to bless and pour out favor, and He *will* work it out. Though Jonah would rather die than obey God, the Lord rescues him. God doesn't say to the fish, "Forget our rescue plan. There's no hope for that sorry rascal. Just let Jonah drown." When God drastically grabs our attention by changing our circumstances, it can be a very shocking experience. In one instant, Jonah goes from facing certain death to finding himself mysteriously still alive. Seaweed is wrapped around Jonah's head. Gastric juices of the fish's stomach are eating away at his skin. Inside that sea creature, he is giving some serious thought to the consequences of disobeying God. What does Jonah finally do?

> Then Jonah prayed to the Lord from inside the fish. (Jonah 2:1)

Good move, Jonah! Way to re-establish communication with God. After three days in the stinky belly of the belching sea creature, Jonah finally concedes. It's about time!

We may be content to lead ourselves in the path of death, but God has something better for us: *life*. Not just any life; a life of obedience.

All along, God directed that fish to swim straight to the place where Jonah should have arrived on his own. Suddenly, the sea creature starts heaving. Vomit spews from the mouth of the fish, and once again, Jonah goes flying through the air. As far as the fish is concerned, Jonah is just a bit too much to swallow.

Landing rear-first on the beach, he stands up. Jonah peers through the seaweed still wrapped around his head. In front of him, he reads a road sign that says, "Nineveh City Straight Ahead."

When God delivers us from the high-risk lifestyle of destructive self-conceit, He does not expect us to return to our old ways. *God's deliverance is designed to return us to* His *destination for our lives*.

What is it that God most often has to deliver us from? In response to our stubborn self will, God goes to great measures to deliver us from the evil of self-absorption and redirect our lives back to His purpose.

A few years ago, God had to rescue me from self-absorption. At the time, I wasn't even aware I needed rescue, but anyone listening to me talk knew I did. In my mind, it was all about *my* family, *my* work, *my* house, *my* this, *my* that. During a security crisis in the country where our family was creatively sharing the gospel, God caused me to be forcibly separated for three months from all things I could classify as *mine*.

After relocating me to a lonely place, God brought me to a point where I clearly saw my need to take self from the center of life and replace self with the Creator God. When I did just that, the storm in my heart quickly came to an end. Before God, I confessed my self-centeredness and surrendered my will to His. In that moment, inner strife was replaced with peace.

Though our family was no longer able to live in the city and province we had come to love, God led us to a different part of the same country, where we focused on migrant workers in factories. Because I had fully surrendered self to whatever God would have me do, the joy of selfless living returned.

Some people believe location doesn't matter, thinking they can serve God wherever they personally choose to live. Through Jonah, God reminds us that our physical location is of great importance to Him. If God wants you to be somewhere, yet you refuse to go, you are being disobedient. Sometimes you are not in the location where God wants you, and you force Him to go to great lengths to relocate you.

Are you where God wants you? Is there an area of your life at high-risk, headed toward self-destruction? What area?

Are you smarter than Jonah?

Question Number Four:

What is the primary thing that causes us to be angry with God?

Jonah wipes the slime off his face and walks into the big city. Everyone smells him coming. They stare at him. *What is this man doing here, and how is it that he came here inside a fish?*

Then Jonah speaks. "People of Nineveh, you are so evil that God says in forty days He will destroy you!"

As he spoke the part about them being destroyed, there was a definite tone of satisfaction in Jonah's voice. He was thinking, *I hope God does destroy you! It will be a pleasure to watch the whole thing. Serves you right—you being so full of yourselves and making me go through a bunch of trouble just to come here and deliver this message to you.*

After speaking to the people, Jonah goes outside the city and finds himself a comfy, outdoor relaxing spot, just as if he were back home. "Go ahead, God. I have my hammock well prepared for comfortable viewing. Let me see you wipe them out, just like I told them you would!"

However, all Jonah sees are people getting on their knees in deeply sorrowful prayer, turning their lives back over to God.

"God, do something now! Wipe them out anyway, just to show them I knew what I was talking about! Come on! I'm watching and waiting! Do it now!" However, God had changed his plans.

> This change of plans upset Jonah, and he became very angry.
> So he complained to the Lord about it: "Didn't I say before I left home that you would do this, Lord? That is why I ran away to Tarshish! I knew that You were a gracious and compassionate God, slow to get angry and filled with unfailing love. I knew how easily You could cancel Your plans for destroying these people.
> "Just kill me now Lord! I'd rather be dead than alive because nothing I predicted is going to happen." (Jonah 4:1–3)

Just how angry is Jonah? He works himself into such an emotional frenzy of pity and rage that he cries out, "Just kill me now Lord! You're *so* embarrassing!"

There he goes again, back to his default mode of operation: self-destructive self-absorption. Why is Jonah angry with God? Because God is not obeying Jonah.

What is the primary reason we get angry with God? Self-absorption. We want God to follow our agenda. We announce that we have given God an agenda and He most certainly will do as we have told Him. When He doesn't, we find Him to be an embarrassment to us. It's then that we'd rather not be associated with Him. He should know better than to cause us to lose face. So we start pouting. We stomp our feet, huff and puff in His face, and remind Him who's the boss.

A father walked into his fifth-grade daughter's room for a chat. When he saw she was praying, he quickly turned and left. Hoping to praise his daughter for what he had seen, the father later asked what she was doing in her room.

She immediately crossed her arms in anger and huffed, "Trying to get God to obey me!"

It turns out she wasn't any smarter than Jonah. Are you smarter than *that* fifth-grader? Check your prayer life. Is most of your prayer time spent asking God to do things for you, for your family, and for your church? Or do you spend most of your time praising God and seeking His direction? Which of these two more adequately describes the way you pray?

- attempting to get God on your agenda
- attempting to get you on God's agenda

By now, it's clear how the "Are You Smarter than Jonah?" game works. It's rigged. For every question, the answers are all the same: I think too much of myself.

Are you *running* from God? Have you become consumed with reaching your own life's destination, while ignoring God's plan for you? Let your *ears* be sensitive to God's voice calling you.

Are you *pacifying* yourself from the exhausting task of fighting life's storms? Depressively sleeping the storm away? While in the eye of storm, make your *eyes* look for God in the storm.

Are you *floundering* in self-depreciation? Needing to be lifted up out of self-made misery? Let God deliver you. Get over a focus on self by getting your *hands* busy serving others.

Are you *pouting* in pity because God isn't doing what you hoped He would do? Overcome pouting by letting your *heart* beat in sync with God's heartbeat.

Self-absorption leads to:	**How to overcome self-absorption**
Running from God	Let my *ears* hear God's call
Pacifying self during the storm	Let my *eyes* focus on God
Floundering in self-depreciation	Let my *hands* be busy serving others
Pouting in pity	Let my *heart* beat with God's heart

The World Revolves Around Me!

OBSESSION: THE CONTROL OF ONE's thought life by an enduring desire, image, or idea. With obsession, the total allegiance of the heart is on the line.

Jonah has an obsession. It's driving him to the point of acting irrationally and harming himself. What is his obsession? Doing drugs? Having illicit sex? Primping his appearance to glowing perfection? Viewing pornography? Is his obsession stealing? Or is it maybe speeding around recklessly in his chariot?

Those things are all surface issues that point to a deeper issue. Jonah's obsession is one of the heart—as is the way with obsessions. Jonah loves *Jonah* more than anything or anyone. He lives in a little world bound on the north, south, east, and west by Jonah. His obsession is self.

Obsessions are heart issues, and they all relate to our fixation on self. We are all Jonah. Of all the obsessions available to us, *self is still the obsession of choice in our generation.*

Popular songs tell us that the greatest love of all is learning to love yourself. The songs are sung so beautifully and made to seem so right. The music of self-love resonates within the soul of every human.

The potentially beautiful symphony we call life has a musical Conductor. When He is given freedom to conduct, the results are fantastic. However, when the musicians start ignoring the Conductor and playing their own tune in their own time, the result is anything but beautiful music. Dancing to the beat of your own drum is not always a good thing.

The promoters of self-love package their product very well. Buyers judge CDs by their covers, but CD covers don't make good music. Stick the disc of self-love into the CD player of life, and the sound that comes out has way too many sour notes. It is certainly not beautiful, even if it has an attractive cover.

That ole rascal named self has even snuck his way into Christianity. He slipped in a side door of the church years ago while no one noticed. Slowly, he shook hands with each person, infecting the Bride of Christ like the swine flu. Through that winsome smile and the boosting of our egos, he won each of us over to thinking of self first.

We have taken what was originally a communal approach to life and made it into something that's all about self. Society says if we are to love our neighbors as ourselves, we must first learn to love ourselves. A popular Christian song leads us to believe that when Jesus died on the cross, he thought of *me* above all.

Though some Christians erroneously teach us to do so, the Bible never commands us to love ourselves. In contrast, the Bible assumes we already do love ourselves. The Bible says we are born in sin.

Doubt that our bent toward self has been with us from birth? Just try getting a two-year-old child to share his favorite toy. Children are naturally selfish. Adults are often just big children.

How many of us brought our newborn baby brother or sister home from the hospital to hear the baby quickly say, "Mommy, how can I help around the house?"

Because we are born with it, a focus on self is something we must unlearn. Is the world really just about me? No. It's about being broken over the sacrifice Jesus made for me while I was surrounding myself in sin. It's about being broken because I am too selfish to share. It's learning to love others as much as I already love myself—that's the challenge! The problem is not that we love ourselves. The problem is that we love only ourselves.

Let's further define self-absorption. It's the *preoccupation with one's own being to the exclusion of others*. One form of self-absorption is "omphaloskepsis," a form of meditation where a person contemplates his or her own navel. We are the "me" generation, staring bug-eyed at our own belly buttons.

For Tessa, our missionary "niece," her reflection was her foe. She developed faster than most girls her age and was the tallest student in her sixth-grade class. Being taller than the boys was something Tessa hated. What boy would like a girl who was taller?

Spending inordinate amounts of time in front of the mirror, Tessa was forever trying to remedy herself. She found nothing but blemishes in the face looking back at her. Examining herself from every possible angle, Tessa wanted to make sure she didn't look ugly from any direction. She would only wear certain outfits because she thought they made her look thinner, so needless to say, her wardrobe was rather small. Excusing herself from the company of family, friends, class, and church, Tessa found a mirror to make sure nothing had changed since the last time she checked. If that isn't vanity, what is?

Jonah knew all about vanity too. He completely missed God's instruction because he was too caught up in himself and what he had going. His vanity led him to escape from his calling because it didn't fit the self-image he wanted.

God wants to save us from a life of self-preoccupation by changing our life's orientation from the kingdom of self to the Kingdom of God. It's not an easy change, but when it happens, the tune played by our lives is in sync with the Conductor. Instead of focusing on self, we look to God and others. We sing in tune and make beautiful music when we follow the Conductor.

If we are to become a part of the larger "we" of life, we must leave the "me" behind. The transformation is not instant. Overcoming "me" can be a long and painful process, as Tessa found. We saw how painful it was for Jonah. There is, within each of us, the default preference of remaining an ugly, self-absorbed monster and choosing to let the monster in the mirror threaten to eat us alive.

How can you know if self-absorption is a problem for you? Any *one* of the following qualifies you as a genuine, certified ego addict.

- Were you born into this world as a human?
- Who do you think about first when you wake up in the morning?
- Who are you thinking about while other people are talking to you?
- When you pray, do you use the words "me" and "my" more than "You" and "Yours?"
- Do you feel powerless to stop thinking about yourself?

In the second chapter, we watched a brief two-minute preview of the Jonah movie. Now, in the rest of the book, we will watch the unedited version of the Jonah movie. It's a full-length, feature presentation. Along the way, we will frequently hit the pause button to allow time for personal function breaks. These breaks will help us apply what is presented. Are you ready to start the movie? Get your popcorn, and punch the play button!

When the world revolves around me, unattainable goals become my pursuit.

> The Lord gave this message to Jonah son of Amittai: Get up and go to the great city of Ninevah! Announce my judgment against it because I have seen how wicked its people are." (Jonah 1:1–2)

God gives Jonah GPS driving directions; however, Jonah doesn't listen to God, his divine GPS (God Positioning System), and finds out the consequences of calling his own shots.

> But Jonah got up and went in the opposite direction in order to get away from the Lord. He went down to the seacoast, to the port of Joppa, where he found a ship leaving for Tarshish. He bought a ticket and went on board, hoping that by going away to the west he could escape from the Lord. (Jonah 1:3)

The moment Jonah starts running from God, he becomes an obsessive-compulsive escape artist. One major wrong turn, and Jonah's journey becomes incredibly long. Jonah's goal of escaping from God is impossible to attain, because no one can hide from God. Running from God only makes the run back to God longer. How frustrating for Jonah!

Many times we tune out God's voice of direction. It is frustrating to hear the GPS say, "Recalculating. Make a legal U-turn." No one likes U-turns. Backtracking wastes time.

Jonah's backtracking definitely costs him time. He buys a ticket from his hometown, Joppa, to Tarshish, which is a little fishing village around Gibraltar on the Atlantic coast of Spain. At that time, a sea voyage from Joppa to Tarshish took almost a year. The ticket also costs him dearly financially. Jonah must be thinking, "Whatever the cost, the farther from Nineveh, the better!"

Are you scurrying off to Tarshish? Your Tarshish is the place to which you run in order to escape from obedience to God. Sometimes you run off in every direction except God's direction.

Jonah's Goal: Run away from God
Jonah's Problem: You can run, but you can't hide!
Jonah's Results:

- His expenses become unbearable: He pays his own fare, and with a year of wasted travel.
- His goals become unachievable: He chases after something impossible to accomplish.

- His determination becomes unquestionable: He runs so furiously that he never stops to ask himself *why* he is running.

When God speaks to a self-centered person, two unhealthy emotions kick in.

- *Fear* says, "That's a scary thing He wants me to do!"
- *Pride* says, "Who does God think I am, His errand boy? I have my own plans, and they don't include going to Nineveh."

The self-absorbed person takes off running like Forrest Gump and refuses to consider letting God deal with the emotions of the heart. The inner voice just keeps saying, "Run, Jonah, run!"

Are you and I running through life without stopping to think about why we are running? It's actually not why we are running that's the question, but from whom we are running. Someone bigger than you wants you to do something for Him, and that scares you. Maybe you are running from your reflection in the mirror, and maybe you are running from your own shadow too. You haven't succeeded in getting away from it yet, though. Maybe you should try to sew your shadow to your shoes like Peter Pan did.

Self-absorption can blind us to the reality that our goals are unattainable. I know this because I am an expert. This book is written about me and for me. You are just along for the ride on Matthew Nance's journey to overcoming my own vanity.

My wife has a brain tumor and is under the care of the Mayo Clinic. She also has an unusual thickening on the stalk of her pituitary stem. What is Matthew thinking about? I *should* be thinking about how much pain my wife is in. I should be concerned with how terrible it must be for her to be out shopping and suddenly get dizzy and fall backwards. Why am I not thinking about how exhausting it is for her to repeatedly become violently nauseous?

Honestly though, I catch myself thinking about how her health situation is affecting me, personally and professionally. Because she is such a great wife, I fear losing even ten percent of the creative brainpower she brings to the marriage team. And I can't help but be concerned about how Cheryl's health might affect my focus on the job.

God is telling me to forget all that and just go with Cheryl into the land of suffering for a season. Instead, I want to run to Tarshish. I want to ignore God's GPS directions taking me to Suffering Street. I don't want the pain for Cheryl or the stress for myself. When obeying becomes this sacrificial, the Jonah in me wants to just run away.

Step off the treadmill of life and stop running for a minute. Get honest with yourself. Is there something or someone you are running from? What, or who, is it?

If you continue running in the same direction you are now going, where will your life end up? What unattainable goals has conceit brought into your life?

Our culture would have us believe that being true to self is a virtue. Jonah shows us that when your world revolves around self, unattainable goals become your pursuit. Being true to self is actually a vice, not a virtue. Be true to God and He will make sure you reach your destiny.

When the world revolves around me, my world begins to spin out of control.

Jonah becomes a very unhappy fugitive from God because of his own willful defiance. He will not listen to God, so God speaks to one who will obey—the wind. The winds of change blow into Jonah's life. God often radically changes the living situation of the self-absorbed person. He does so to get our attention and show us how futile our attempts are at forging our own path. The Jonah in me thinks I have everything under control, but a life of self-conceit spins itself out of control.

> But as the ship was sailing along, suddenly the Lord flung a powerful wind over the sea, causing a violent storm that threatened to send them to the bottom. (Jonah 1:4)

What or who does your world revolve around? What areas of your life are spinning out of control?

When the world revolves around me, other people are affected by my high-risk lifestyle.

> Fearing for their lives, the desperate sailors shouted to their gods for help and threw the cargo overboard to lighten the ship. (Jonah 1:5a)

Those who hang out with a self-obsessed person are at equally high risk. If you are associated with a navel gazer, you better increase your insurance coverage!

What does your life feel like to those around you? Do the stormy winds of your life make them seasick? Let's look at what the storm looked like to the sailors on Jonah's ship.

As the waves are blowing clear across the deck of the tossing ship, the desperate sailors move with adrenaline-amped speed. They throw overboard everything they can grab. We see the true value of material possessions when danger or death threatens.

These are tough, bold sailors who are not easily overcome with fear. However, the storm is so great, these Phoenician seamen realize they need spiritual help. They begin calling on their idols and trinket gods to save them.

Imagine one sailor pulling from his pocket a tooth that came from his great-great grandpa's mouth. "Oh spirit of my ancestor, I beg you! Help me chomp my way out of this storm!"

Pulling a rabbit's foot out of his pocket, one sailor prays, "Spirit of the lucky white rabbit, help me hop off this boat!"

Another prays to his wooden, hand-carved, sexy sea goddess. "My mermaid savior, swim back to me real fast, baby. I need you now more than ever!"

Each man prays to his own little god for salvation. No one prays to the one true God. Such is the futility of the human in crisis, hopelessly depending on manmade voodoo.

You may not have let self-absorption become the terrible storm that it was for the sailors, but you may have some smaller storm in your life causing danger to those around you. Tessa caused a storm for her family during her mirror years. As she lashed out, was moody, and became withdrawn, Tessa made her family suffer the consequences of her self-centeredness. Somehow everything seemed to be her parent's fault.

Self-absorption blinds you to the reality of the trouble you are causing others. You don't realize you are hurting family and friends because you are too busy worrying about yourself.

Who is at risk in your life? Why?

When the world revolves around me, I withdraw from reality and am lulled into my own sleepy world.

While the sailors scramble for survival, Jonah is blissfully unaware of the impending danger and that he is the cause for the storm. Where is he, anyway?

Jonah makes no attempt to help the crew. He couldn't care less about them. While the sailors are throwing cargo overboard and praying to a pantheon of gods, what is Jonah doing? Sleeping! What should Jonah be doing? He should be praying to the one true God. *When God allows tribulation in my life, He expects me to tribulate, not sleep!* Jonah should confess his sin so the storm could stop. However, Jonah can't call on the help of the One he was trying to ignore.

> And all this time Jonah was sound asleep down in the hold. (Jonah 1:5b)

Jonah erroneously thinks, "I have done the right thing. I have peace within. I have been true to myself. I will just let my conscience be my guide. The thing to do now is reward myself. I have suffered a traumatic ordeal. Now I have finally put myself out of harm's way, and out of God's way. Well done, self! I deserve a break today. I should take a nap!"

Jonah goes into a deep sleep. Refusing to follow God's will is exhausting. Our culture tells us to hang loose. It convinces us to shirk responsibility and never feel guilty. Society would like us to believe our problems are never our responsibility.

Pretending there is no storm takes a greater toll on us than facing the storm. Like Jonah, neither the storm around you nor your own guilty conscience disturbs your false sense of security. Your feeling can deceive you and keep you from accurately evaluating whether or not you are running from God.

Imagine being haunted by ghosts. The ghost of self-absorption flies through the wall to spook us. He takes us back to the trail of empty beer bottles from the nights we used alcohol to feel numb.

Gluttony the ghost waddles over. He prompts our memory of all the candy, French fries, and ice cream we gorged ourselves on to alleviate our troubles.

The next ghost whisks us to a bathroom littered with empty pill bottles. Remember the painkillers popped? Or maybe it was actually hard drugs.

Lust, our next ghost, uncovers the nest of Playboy magazines strategically placed in hidden corners under our bed and under our pile of dirty clothes.

Shopping binges and credit card overages do not escape the next ghost's attention, as she shows us the movie set of *Confessions of a Shopaholic*. This time, we are the stars of the film.

All of these ghosts remind us our own tendency toward selfishly withdrawing from the difficult things God would have us do.

When the storms of life come, where do you go? Which of the ghosts do you run to?

When the world revolves around me, withdrawal from reality lulls me into my own little sleepy world.

When the world revolves around me, self-destruction may eventually become my desire.

A storm is about to sink the ship. Jonah is fast asleep. What happens next?

Jonah rubs the sleep out of his eyes. The captain is shaking him to wake him up. As Jonah stumbles up the steps to the deck of the ship, he is told to draw a straw, along with everyone else on board. He hears one sailor say, "One of us has upset the gods. The one who draws the shortest straw is to blame for the storm."

> So the captain went down after him. "How can you sleep at a time like this?" he shouted. "Get up and pray to your god! Maybe he will have mercy on us and spare our lives." (Jonah 1:6)

> Then the crew cast lots to see which of them had offended the gods and caused the terrible storm. When they did this, Jonah lost the toss.
>
> "What have you done to bring this awful storm down on us?" they demanded. "Who are you? What is your line of work? What country are you from? What is your nationality?" (Jonah 1:7–8)

Jonah draws the shortest straw. Suddenly the sailors direct all of their attention to him.

"You! You're the one that brought on this disaster! Who are you? Why are you on board? What in the world have you done to upset the gods?"

> And Jonah answered, "I am a Hebrew, and I worship the Lord, the God of Heaven, who made the sea and the land." Then he told them that he was running away from the Lord.
>
> The sailors were terrified when they heard this. "Oh, why did you do it?" they groaned. (Jonah 1:9–10)

The sailors knew everyone on board except for Jonah. Why? Jonah had concealed his identity. Finally, he had no choice but to fess up.

Jonah tells them he is a Jew and he's running away from God. The sailors have heard of Jonah's God, and they are scared nuts.

> And since the storm was getting worse all the time, they asked him, "What should we do to you to stop this storm?"
>
> "Throw me into the sea," Jonah said, "and it will become calm again. For I know this terrible storm is my fault." (Jonah 1:11–12)

"Throw me overboard. I want to end my miserable life," Jonah says. "There's nothing to live for anymore."

Jonah almost gets his wish.

When you are full of yourself, you have no way of making decisions that are bigger than the moment. There is nothing more to life than "me" and "now." This is ultimately what brings Jonah down. His immediate decisions trap him in a corner.

The ghosts come back once again to haunt us. The next ghost shows us all the harmful things we did to our body, how we disrespected it with trashy clothes and abused it with razor blades and bulimia.

The ghost of self-hatred appears after the next bell toll. This ghost positions us in front of a mirror and reminds us of everything we found wrong with ourselves, on the inside and outside. With a permanent marker, the ghost guides our hand to circle every blemish. The ghost of self-hatred can lead to low self-esteem, anorexia, bulimia, and even suicide.

The ghost of self-absorption shows us his subtle side. He doesn't inflict physical pain, but the mental anguish is slow and gradual. We don't even notice its onslaught.

What areas of your life show evidence of self-destructive tendencies?

When the world revolves around me, self-destruction may become my eventual desire.

When the world revolves around me, the rest of the world can't stand having me around.

At first, the sailors are not willing to throw Jonah overboard. But there seems to be no other alternative. No matter how hard they row, the boat isn't moving. Finally one of the sailors grabs Jonah by the arms, and another sailor grabs his feet. They carry him to the edge of the ship and start swinging. His body gathers momentum to fly over the side of the ship on the count of, "One, two, thr—!"

> Instead, the sailors tried even harder to row the boat ashore. But the stormy sea was too violent for them, and they couldn't make it. Then they cried out to the Lord, Jonah's God. "O Lord," they pleaded, "don't make us die for this man's sin. And don't hold us responsible for his death, because it isn't our fault. O Lord, You have sent this storm upon him for Your own good reasons." (Jonah 1:13–14)

"Hey, stop! Before we toss him overboard, don't you think we ought to pray to his God?" one sailor says. "We might, you know, have a little funeral service for the poor guy. Otherwise the storm might continue!"

One of the sailors takes his hat off and places it on his heart. The others do the same. He clears his throat and begins an awkward prayer. "Uh, well, you see Great One, it's like this. What we're about to do here is not our fault. Jonah, Thy self-absorbed prophet, caused Thee to send this storm.

So, Thou surely canst cut us some slack 'bout tossing him overboard to end this here storm. Bless Jonah's soul as he drowns now Lord, and we ask that Thou ain't gonna hold what we're 'bout to do 'gainst us. Guess that'll 'bout do it, God. Uh, well, Amen, then."

As much as those sailors hate to do it, they just can't stand having Jonah around anymore, so they toss him overboard.

> Then the sailors picked Jonah up and threw him into the raging sea, and the storm stopped at once! (Jonah 1:15)

Self-absorbed people often get a negative reaction from others. Being obsessed with yourself turns you into a selfish, lonely person, cut off from others. When you are focused on self to the neglect of God and others, no one wants to have you around.

Take Bart and Shaba as examples.

- Bart is a self-absorbed friend. He dominates the conversation and doesn't understand why people keep making excuses to walk away from him when he is still talking.
- Shaba is a high-maintenance spouse. She takes from the relationship whatever she feels she is entitled to. Her husband tries to keep her happy, but now he is so fed up with her that he's packing his bags. She blames the bitter end of their relationship on his insensitivity.

J. Oswald Sanders says, "Egotism is one of the repulsive manifestations of pride. It is the practice of thinking and speaking much of oneself, the habit of magnifying one's attainments or importance. It leads one to consider everything in its relation to himself rather than in relation to God and the welfare of His people."[7]

In your relationships with others, what percentage of the relationship revolves around you?

When the world revolves around me, the rest of the world can't stand having me around.

Ready for a joke?

Question: How many Jonahs does it take to change a light bulb?

Answer: Only one. He just stands there and holds the light bulb, since the whole world already revolves around him!

This world actually revolves around the One who created it. He made you to revolve around Him. You must get to know Him personally through Jesus Christ. You must serve God by serving others. There you will find what Jonah never did—the true, lasting joy of really living.

What will you do this week to say yes to God's call of reaching out beyond self to serve others?

Life is not about me. It never has been and never will be. Whenever I pretend it's all about me, I create a world that's far too small and boring. I may even become whale barf!

What if God called you to move into an inner-city apartment complex in order to reach the people who live there? It probably wouldn't be the part of town you'd choose. However, think of the new challenges, new relationships, and new spiritual blessings that could be yours from saying yes to God.

How is your life making a difference in the Kingdom of God? How is your life making a difference in the lives of other people? The life worth living is all about serving God through serving others, so if you are not serving, what are you doing?

Even when you are disobedient, you can't stop God's will from being accomplished. Because of Jonah, the men on the boat begin worshipping the true God. Jonah's disobedience brings trouble, but it also brings the repentance of an entire crew.

> The sailors were awestruck by the Lord's great power, and they offered Him a sacrifice and vowed to serve Him. (Jonah 1:16)

After the sailors throw Jonah overboard and the storm suddenly stops, God uses Jonah despite his own resistance. Everyone Jonah meets repents. The only one not happy about this is Jonah. When he goes into the water, Jonah nearly drowns in self-pity, wishing he were dead. However, as we will see in the next chapter, Jonah gets one more chance. Do not miss the chance that God is now giving you to look beyond self and see the bigger picture.

It is by looking up and looking out rather than merely looking inward that you begin to see how you can become more than just yourself.

One Whale of a Jail!

The Ego Addict's Twelve Steps to Prison Break

Let's see, where did we leave off? Oh yes, Jonah is flying through the air. He's been tossed from the ship and he's ready to die.

He never imagines that he would somehow be rescued from drowning. Jonah simply feels himself sinking deep in the water, knowing that his life is over. He can't hold his breath much longer and his eyeballs already feel like they are going to explode.

Suddenly, Jonah sees a sea monster approaching in the distance! The huge fish's mouth is open and Jonah is horrified. The fish breathes in, and there goes Jonah, down the hatch, all in one big gulp. He's in one whale of a jail.

Imagine how miserable Jonah must be inside the fish. Seaweed is wrapped around his head. The fish's digestive juices are beginning to turn him into a prune. He is in solitary confinement in the pitch-black belly of a stinking fish. God has put Jonah in time out.

We'd all agree that whales don't have windows, but there is a spiritual window that God gives Jonah: a three-day window of opportunity for an attitude adjustment.

Why does Jonah need an attitude adjustment? We already know it is Jonah's ego that has him in the belly of the whale. Ken Blanchard has defined ego, E-G-O, as **E**dging **G**od **O**ut.[8] That's exactly what Jonah has done, and as a result, he's in a whale of trouble!

What is your whale?
- Low self-esteem
- Debt
- Laziness
- Pornography
- Hopelessness
- Living like a slob
- Craving more power, money, food
- Taking advantage of others

- Sex, drugs, or alcohol
- Unfulfilling relationships
- Depression

Have you weathered a storm at heart? Have you been thrown overboard and nearly drowned? Now you are living all alone in the belly of a whale with resentment, bitterness, an unforgiving spirit, and self-condemnation. You can't live but you are not dead, either—you are comatose.

You may feel like a whale has swallowed you and there's no way out of your dilemma. Is every day a Jonah day? Are you struggling for survival, yet drowning in hopelessness? Tired of fighting? Ready to surrender?

Sadly, many of us stay in this situation much longer than Jonah did. Jonah was in his jail for only three days. Some of us have been stuck in a stench of our own making for years. We can't see and don't know how to get out. We just keep living hemmed in on every side, trying not to be eaten up by the beast that has swallowed us.

Understand this: it is not God's will for you to live permanently inside a fish. It is not His will for you to be comatose. Deliverance is available and is waiting for you to accept it. However, you first need to recognize the fish you are trapped in. Take a deep whiff. It stinks in the fish. Life doesn't have to be this way. The question is, do you want it to be different?

If you've made a mess of life while running from God, you are not alone. We've all been there and done that. The question is, how can you be delivered out of the prison of your own making? How is Jonah delivered? Come along as we follow Jonah to an Ego Addicts Anonymous (EAA) meeting, where we'll learn the twelve-step program for breaking out of the prison of self-absorption.

At first no one is talking in the EAA meeting. People with ego problems do not talk *with* other people; they only talk *to* other people. After a minute or so, one young man finally breaks the uncomfortable silence.

"Hello, my name is Jonah, and I'm an ego addict."

"Hello, Jonah."

Jonah smiles and says, "From my experience, I want to tell you the twelve steps to a prison break from self-destructive egotism."

Step One: Be done with prayer-less living

Jonah says, "Just how far down was I willing to go before I finally called on the Lord? All the way to the bottom of the sea! Even then, it took me awhile to pray to the God I had rejected. When we make a mess of things, why don't we pray? Why is prayer saved as a last resort, when we decide there's nothing else left to do but pray?"

> Now the Lord had arranged for a great fish to swallow Jonah. And Jonah was inside the fish for three days and three nights. *Then* Jonah prayed ... (Jonah 1:17–2:1) [Emphasis mine]

Sometimes we think we have no right to call on God. We mistakenly think if we were to call on Him, He wouldn't listen to us because of bad things we've done. "I've been so bad God couldn't possibly still love me." Does that sound familiar?

Maybe we don't pray because we are too proud. We think we've made it through bad things before without bothering God and we can make it this time too. Are we trying to impress God and others by faking them all out with a false front? "I'm doing just fine". Really?

We tend to be self-reliant, and this keeps us from praying. So many people stay stuck and never call on God for help, thinking they've got a few more tricks up their sleeve before they are ready to throw in the towel. But honestly, how many tricks do we have?

In the Ego Addicts meeting, Jonah speaks to us again. "I finally admitted, 'God, unless You come through for me, I'm sunk!' Inside the fish, I prayed, 'God, you gave me this nice little three-day retreat where all I can do is pray. Now God, this isn't exactly a long weekend at the spa.'"

If you do not make time for prayer with God, He will make time for you. "If God, in His grace, finds no other means of making us honor Him among men, He will cast us in the deep," Charles Spurgeon, a famous British pastor, wrote.[9]

Jonah lives prayer-less until it almost kills him, then he finally prays. Some people wait until they are on the edge of death to cry out to God. Though they may have missed the blessing of a life of faithfully serving God and others, God is there at death's door waiting for the one who cries out to Him. It's never too late to pray.

Be done with prayer-less living. Stop reserving prayer for emergencies only. Pray continually. Talk to God like He's one of your friends. He is, after all, the best kind of confidant—He won't go spilling out all your secrets.

Make conversation with God a way of life when making daily decisions. If you do this, you will discover your emergencies will lessen.

Step Two: Cry out to God for help

Jonah prays from inside the whale. Notice carefully what he says in His prayer. He recalls the time prior to being saved by the fish. Jonah remembers how he sank down to the bottom of the water and on the way down he called out to God for salvation. Note that Jonah's prayer is one from the heart, not a verbal prayer. Jonah would have drowned had he opened his mouth to verbally pray! He may not be able to verbalize his prayer, but Jonah thanks God for hearing the prayer of his heart.

> Jonah prayed to the Lord his God from inside the fish. He said, "I cried out to the Lord in my great trouble, and He answered me. I called to you from the world of the dead, and Lord, you heard me!"
> (Jonah 2:1–2)

He tells God that He's got his attention—and it's a good thing too, since he is milliseconds away from drowning. That's when God, full of wonderful surprises, delivers Jonah in a most unexpected way. A fish interrupts Jonah's prayer and swallows him whole.

God is full of surprises. Don't make God small by thinking he couldn't possibly have a solution to your problem. And guess what—He gives second chances if you mess up on the first. Be grateful for these second chances.

Crying out requires us to admit we can't do anything to save ourselves, and that is a bit hard to swallow sometimes. Crying out requires humility. Humility is hard because we don't want to be reliant on someone else. But crying out in a storm allows God to bless us with grace.

No matter how dark life may seem, do not give up. Pray for help. Hold on, and cry out to Him for deliverance.

Step Three: Accept life's storms as a means of receiving God's grace

At the Ego Addicts meeting, Jonah says, "I didn't just pray, 'God, the storm was a fluke of nature. It was bad luck.' No, when I prayed, I gave God full credit for all the crazy things that have happened to me. I know there is such a thing as an act of God because I was in the belly of one of God's greater acts!"

> You threw me into the ocean depths, and I sank down to the heart of the sea. I was buried beneath your wild and stormy waves. (Jonah 2:3)

Jonah actually is appreciative that God allowed him to be in this miserable state. He knows it could be worse—he could be dead. It isn't comfortable being in the belly of a whale. It's not easy to appreciate being uncomfortable, but these things bring us to a place of obedience.

Like Jonah, we seek comfort. God seeks obedience. These two opposing forces often produce violent storms. In His grace, just as He did with Jonah, God brings us down to the point where we are ready for a needed attitude adjustment.

When God brings Jonah down off his pedestal, Jonah doesn't look at everything he has lost, nor does he dwell on the dark prison surrounding him. He looks out through the window of opportunity and sees God's sovereign hand at work in his circumstances.

Remember, there is always a window. Windows aren't doors though. Windows show us there is a way out, and they show us that God will open a door if we acknowledge the window He has provided.

God allows you to experience what it's like to be trapped in a prison. It is there that you become willing to let go of life lived for self. Seeing the window reminds you there is a world outside your prison.

Sure, Satan wants to keep us in a whale of a jail. However, he cannot stop the prison-breaking power of prayer. See God's hand at work in the storm of your current circumstances and accept the storm as a means of bringing you into God's grace. Sure, it is frustrating to have confining circumstances. Hitting rock bottom is not a comfortable experience. However, it is there that God is able to get your attention.

Step Four: Recognize I am far away from God

People in the Ego Addict's circle lean closer to hear what Jonah says. He continues, "A whale's stomach is not a place anyone would choose to live. It is, however, a healthy place to learn the truth about self. God did not heal my heart until I realized that my heart was sick. God heals when we recognize how far we are away from Him."

> Then I said, "O Lord, You have driven me from your presence. How will I ever again see your holy temple? (Jonah 2:4)

In the fish, Jonah gets so low that he realizes he is far away from God. Instead of desiring to flee from God, he now longs to be close to God. It sometimes takes a speeding ticket to get us to slow down. In hard times, I am still and quiet long enough to realize what God has already done for me. Sometimes I don't realize what I have until I've lost it. It's in the losing that I see my circumstances in a new light. Then, self-absorption begins to fade.

Jonah dreams of worshipping the Lord in His temple in Jerusalem. As he looks death in the face, the possibility of going back to Jerusalem seems like an impossible dream. What is your Jerusalem? What place or times in your life are you trying to get back to?

It's easier to get back where you were when you recognize where you are now. Jonah honestly recognizes how far he has run from God and has faith that somehow he will make it back to Israel. In humility, Jonah reconnects with God. Though he is surrounded by seaweed, Jonah now has a strong sense that God's presence is surrounding him.

It also helps to recognize the source of our problems. Sure, the mere presence of evil in this world brings much trouble and sometimes other people really are the source of trouble. However, most of our troubles come about because of our own disobedience.

It's interesting that we don't tend to say that we are far from God. Rather, we say that God is far from us. Jonah rightly discerns that he is where he is because of what he has done. He is the one who separated himself from God.

What does it take for you to admit the great distance between God and self-absorbed you? Will it take a trauma that separates you from feeling secure within yourself? Sometimes, you need to be tossed overboard. It may take a storm and a fish. Often it takes a hospital bed, depression, or a close call with death. After an experience beyond our control, we become serious about living for the Lord.

Is there a part of you that is far away from God? How have you been disobedient? Your body can be in God's temple, yet your heart still may be in rebellion. Humbly and honestly, you must get reconnected to God.

Step Five: Admit I am powerless to help myself

The group of Ego Addicts is startled as Jonah says, "The old Jonah deceived himself into thinking I knew better than God. The new Jonah admits the mess I made of things."

> I sank beneath the waves, and death was very near. The waters closed in around me, and seaweed wrapped itself around my head. I sank down to the very roots of the mountains. I was locked out of life and imprisoned in the land of the dead. (Jonah 2:5–6)

As you and I listen in on Jonah at the meeting, we recognize that we are powerless to help ourselves. Have we reached the point of becoming open to God's help? Once inside the belly of the whale, we are powerless and forced to be still and listen. There is nothing else we can do. It's not like there is Internet or anything there in the fish's belly.

Why do we need to be forced to listen? It's because you and I are ego addicts. We are imprisoned by our own feeling of self-importance. It takes an act of God to pull the cotton balls out of our ears. We must realize we are just as powerless as Jonah to free ourselves. What must we do? Desire freedom from ego addiction, and be willing to surrender your will to His. He will release the chains that bind you.

Christianity is not a works-based religion. You can't work your way out of a whale of a jail. The way you find freedom is to surrender, not fight. Surrender takes humility. For some reason, today humility carries negative connotations.

Jonah won't surrender, and that's how he ends up in a whale. For some of us, it often takes multiple miserable experiences before we admit we should be true to God. We may be imprisoned by different struggles at different times in our lives. Obedience is a lifelong process. Hopefully, after learning from past experiences, we will be able to recognize the opportunity to surrender before we get to the point of being swallowed by a whale.

Do you recognize how far down you've gone? Do you accept the reality that self-help is not the way out?

Step Six: Pray the Word of God

There's something quite remarkable about Jonah's prayer. He does not pray anything original. Everything he says is a quote from Scripture. He quotes the Bible eight times.

In Jonah 2:2, he quotes Psalm 18:6. "But in my distress I cried out to the Lord; yes, I prayed to my God for help." He also quotes Psalm 86:13, "You have rescued me from the depths of death."

Open your Bible and take a look at how Jonah has memorized and is meditating on the word of God as he prays.

Jonah 2:3	Psalm 88:6
Jonah 2:4	Psalm 31:22
Jonah 2:5	Psalm 69:1-2
Jonah 2:6	Psalm 30:3

Jonah tells the Ego Addicts group about how he prayed. "When I was a child, my father helped me memorize scripture. I know the words of God and found it easy to simply pray the words of God back to Him. I found that praying the word of God causes *Him* to increase and *self* to decrease."

Memorizing God's Word is absolutely vital for survival in "belly of the whale" experiences. When you are going through a hard time, quoting Scripture to yourself reminds you of God's promises and presence. It can pull you through.

It is crucial to have a Biblical basis for your hope and faith. Do you know why you have hope? Do you know what you believe, and can you support it with Bible verses? Are you ready to encourage someone else by praying the Scriptures for them?

During "Jonah" days, read the Bible. You will find that you are not the first person to spend time in the belly of a whale. There are plenty of other people in the Bible who've been stuck in stinky places.

Look for verses that can easily be expressed to God in prayer. Pray the word of God—and never, ever underestimate the power of prayer.

Step Seven: Look to the Lord for my deliverance

God is at work delivering you! He has not forgotten you. Do not believe the lie of some who say God forgets or turns His back on people. "For I know the plans I have for you," says the Lord. "They are plans for good and not for disaster, to give you a future and a hope." (Jeremiah 29:11)

> But you, o Lord, my God, have snatched me from the yawning jaws of death! (Jonah 2:6)

What is God specifically doing right now to save you from your own self-destructive tendencies? Though you may have been a busy bandit running from God, God is chasing after you. For your own good, He arrests you, but just long enough to bring you to your senses. He is working hard to bring all men back to Himself.

The "I did it my way" approach ignores God as our deliverer. Doing it your way circumvents blessings, and it usually means, "I did it the harder way."

Jonah is not saved from the whale to live as he pleases. He is released to serve. We are delivered from slavery to serve our Savior. We serve our Savior when we serve the body of Christ and those who don't believe yet. He wants us to use our talents to serve others, all for the glory of God.

Step Eight: Direct my mind off myself and onto the Lord

When things are just mildly bad, we still think of self. That's when we reward ourselves by throwing a pity party and inviting sympathy from friends and loved ones. However, when things get really, really bad, we realize we can't do anything to save ourselves. How awesome would it be to realize this before things get really, really bad?

> When I had lost all hope, I turned my thoughts once more to the Lord. And my earnest prayer went to You in Your holy temple. (Jonah 2:7)

The people in the addict's circle ask Jonah to say more. So he says, "When I had lost all hope in surviving, it was like time stood still. I had a flashback to worshipping the Lord in the temple. After refusing to think about God for so long, in that moment of panic my thoughts turned back to the Lord. How eager God is to rescue those whose thoughts turn to Him!"

In the fish, Jonah realizes his impotence and starts concentrating on God. He starts listening instead of talking. He remembers God's faithfulness, love, mercy, and miraculous power to deliver. Jonah begins visualizing himself outside of the fish and worshipping God in the temple in Jerusalem.

God has designed the storm in your life to take your old self down to a watery grave. There is no possibility to make it through unless God intervenes. Then, He will graciously let you come back up to the surface to breathe in newness of life.

Step Nine: Give up idols

Jonah says to the circle of fellow strugglers, "Just before I was thrown overboard to die, I saw the sailors calling on their idols to calm the storm. The storm kept raging, even though they ranted and raved for their gods to save them. I know that only the true God answers prayer."

> Those who worship false gods turn their backs on all God's mercies. (Jonah 2:8)

After choking back deep emotions, Jonah continues. "I have felt the emptiness of clinging to the worthless idol of self. Now, I want to experience the joy of close fellowship with the Lord and obedience to His will."

What are the things to which you devote more time and energy than you do to God? Among the things you would have to give up, what would be the most difficult thing in your life to lose?

An idol is anything that is more important to you than God, even if it is a good thing. Be done with self-serving idols.

Step Ten: Praise God, even in the midst of the crisis

> But I will offer sacrifices to You with my songs of praise. (Jonah 2:9)

If Jonah can sing praises from the belly of a fish, surely we can put on the garment of praise in the midst of our distress.

We can tell a lot about a person by whether or not they are willing to sing praises to God in hard times. Some praise Him only when things are going well. Those who learn to praise Him in the storm find their hearts renewed.

Feeling down in the dumps? Make a gratitude list. Write down everything you are thankful about, and see how much better you feel. Listen to praise music, and sing along. Start praising God. Praising God diverts the attention from self to God. Believe it or not, moping and pouting really doesn't feel good or get you anywhere. It takes more muscles to frown than it does to smile.

Step Eleven: Renew my vow to live in obedience to God

Obedience is a lifelong process. Let's rejoin Ego Addicts Anonymous and hear what Jonah has to say. "I started visualizing myself outside the fish and promising God all I would do after getting out," says Jonah.

> I will fulfill all my vows. For my salvation comes from the Lord alone. (Jonah 2:9)

There is a price to pay for freedom from the jail of self-absorption. There is no "get out of jail free" card. The price of freedom from egotism is radical obedience to God.

Neither the sailors nor the storm can make Jonah willing to go to Nineveh. Finally, what makes Jonah willing to obey is living in a fish for three days. You'd think it'd be hard to forget an experience like that. Well, Jonah does forget, but we'll get to how that happened later in the book.

In the fish, Jonah thinks back to how God commanded him to go to Nineveh, and Jonah decides he is now ready to go there. He's ready to go *anywhere* outside of that stinking fish!

When you are suffering because of your own disobedience, you must admit that you are wrong and return to the Lord. Are you running from God?

Before you began running from God, what was the last command God gave you?

Go back to that command. Are you now willing to obey? Then make a solemn vow to God that you will obey what He said to do. Sometimes this vow will need to be renewed. You will be tempted to forget all that God did for you.

Step Twelve: Think outside the Fish![10]

The fish gets a terrible stomachache. He has had all of Jonah he can swallow. Jonah's heart has become closer to God, and the fish is feeling queasy, knowing that you can't keep a good man down. The beast vomits Jonah out. Once again, Jonah goes flying through the air, only this time he lands on dry ground. He is now on the solid ground of obedience. The man that the fish regurgitates is a much wiser man than the one it swallowed.

> Then the Lord ordered the fish to spit up Jonah on the beach, and it did. (Jonah 2:10)

The fish was a dungeon, but only a temporary one. It soon becomes a free ride to the place of obedience to God's will. Jonah basks in the sunshine on the beach and likely takes the time to debrief his amazing experience, writing down what we now have in the portion of our Bibles called Jonah Chapter 2.

Why does God rescue Jonah? It's not just to keep Jonah from drowning. It is so the people of Nineveh could be saved from drowning in sin. Look beyond your current darkness. There is no such thing as a hopeless case. God has a great purpose for your life! It's time to think outside the fish. God rescues you from a lifestyle of self-centeredness for the purpose of using you in selfless evangelism and missions. You have looked at what God is delivering you *from*. Now you must ask yourself, for what purpose is God delivering you?

Perhaps for some of us, deliverance may still seem impossible. Some feel hopelessly trapped. Begin to see the situation from a different angle. Picture yourself as if you are already outside the fish. Visualize God delivering you from your self-made prison. Think about the new person you will become through God's power. Though it may seem like only a dream, talk to yourself, to the Lord, and to others about the specific ways that things are going to be different for you sooner than later. You've been in a whale of a jail long enough already!

Failure Is Not Final!

Discover the God of Second Chances

At 3:26 p.m. on Thursday, January 15, 2009, U.S. Airways flight 1549 took off from LaGuardia Airport in New York with 150 passengers and five crew members. Suddenly, a flock of Canadian geese were sucked into the engines, causing at least one engine to catch on fire. The plane began to drop rapidly.

Seated in the back row, Vallie Collins texted her family. "The plane is crashing. We're going to die."

The pilot's voice came on. There was only time for one sentence to be spoken: "Brace for impact." Pilot and copilot spotted the Hudson River and instantly began to guide the plane down onto the water. Such a landing is exceptionally tricky, with a high possibility of the plane doing cartwheels or nose diving down into the water. People on board believed their lives were over.

Against all odds, the plane landed smoothly on top of the water. However, water began rapidly filling the plane. People in the back of the plane were waist deep in water.

Amazingly, nearby commuter ferries and tugboats arrived within seconds, and the US Coast Guard arrived within minutes. Everyone on board flight 1549 was saved. Though shaken by the trauma, all 155 people on board were given a second chance at life.

God is all about giving us second chances—just ask Jonah. Though Jonah is thrown overboard during a storm, God is not willing to let Jonah die. Jonah had willfully defied God. God said go, and Jonah said no. Would God respond to Jonah by striking him down with a bolt of lightning from heaven?

Despite Jonah's self-centered rebellion, God still has something He wants done through Jonah. Though man ignores God and even profanes His name, God is like a heavenly hound continuing to chase after man.

Sometimes people make foolish mistakes. When Jesus needed him most, Peter denied he even knew the Lord. Later, though Jesus had told Peter to become a fisher of men, Peter instead reverted back to simply fishing for fish rather than men. It was then that the resurrected Jesus appeared to Peter and said, "Peter, do you love me?"

"Yes, Lord, you know that I love you."

"Then feed my sheep." Jesus affirmed that despite his failures, Peter was still useful to God's kingdom.

Do you find yourself living life at a level far below what was originally designed for you? Are you asking, *Has God put me on the sidelines of life? Will God ever use me again? Does He even care about me anymore?* The answer: "Yes! He cares deeply about you."

Satan would have us think that failure is final, but God has gone to drastic measures to say it isn't so. He even allowed His own Son to die for you to remind you that He is not through with you yet. He gives you a second chance.

Sometimes we are so self absorbed that we don't even realize there is a possibility of getting a second chance at life. You may think, *There's nothing that can be done to change my life at this point. I have been the way I am for so long. Change is just not possible.*

Think again! We may have given up on the possibility of circumstances ever changing, but one thing about God: He is full of surprises. God has not given up on us. Regardless of where you have been or what you have done, He is still a God of second chances. When you see a second chance, take it.

Take a Second Chance for Personal Obedience

> Then the Lord spoke to Jonah a *second* time. "Get up and go to the great city of Nineveh, and deliver the message of judgment I have given you." (Jonah 3:1–2)

How amazing that God speaks to Jonah a second time! Let's pretend that Mr. Jonah is employed in a modern day company. His boss assigns him the task of going to the Middle East. So what does Jonah do? He takes off for the Bahamas! Would his boss give him a second chance? No way! Mr. Jonah would be fired immediately.

Not so with God. God forgets all about Jonah's terrible failure. The Lord does not hold against Jonah the fact that Jonah is running from God. He actively runs after Jonah, tackles him down to the ground, and says, "Jonah, let's give it another try now. Get up and go to Nineveh this time."

I am Jonah. You are also Jonah. We have been through it all; cast overboard, left to die, fallen to the depths of despair, and gotten stuck in the stinking belly of moping and groping through life. God says to us, "Get up and go! I have an important purpose to fulfill through your life. I'm giving you a second chance, so get out there and get after it."

The offer of a second chance is not enough. You and I must *take* the chance. We must respond with obedience. Say yes to God's offer to put you back in service to Him. Seize the God-given opportunity to joyfully obey Him.

I hear you saying, *I've already missed out on what God wants for my life. It's too late now.* No! Don't say what isn't true. There is still another chance; take it.

Moses killed an Egyptian and fled from Egypt. God chased after him and called Moses to become a great leader. Failure, even for a murderer, is not final. When we fail, God doesn't give up on us.

> This time Jonah obeyed the Lord's command and went to Nineveh … (Jonah 3:3)

God speaks a second time to Jonah, "Get up and go!" This time, what does Jonah do? He gets up and goes God's way. Early in the drama, we see self-absorbed Jonah getting up to run away from God. Later, while Jonah is in the belly of the fish, he is running to God. And now we see Jonah finally running *with* God.

The first time Jonah heard God's voice, he didn't think that God had Jonah's best interest in mind. So he ran from God. However, God then caused Jonah to barely escape death, and suddenly God has a more cooperative Jonah.

Earlier, Jonah had thought, "What could be more ludicrous than obeying God? What could be more fun than a cruise to Tarshish?" Jonah is about to get the answer to his question: going to Nineveh and seeing the surprising results of obeying God![11] The truly happy people of this world are those who obediently and adventurously go wherever God's sends them.

> …Jonah…went to Nineveh, a city so large that it took three days to see it all. (Jonah 3:3)

Taking a second chance at obeying God does not mean things will get easier. Jonah finds out that obeying God involves much danger and hard work. On arriving at Nineveh, Jonah might write something like this in his spiritual journal:

Here I am God! I've traveled hundreds of miles just to get here. Wow! Nineveh is a huge city! And You do remember, don't You God, that Nineveh is the headquarters of the most cruel nation on the planet? The kings of Nineveh cut off the noses of the people they conquer, and while they are still alive, they peel off their skin![12]

Jonah might write this as well.

Lord, I want to remind you that I have obediently come into the center of our nation's most hated enemy. You want me to march around this city telling them they are doomed for destruction? Do You realize the potential occupational hazards of my doing so? Is my life insurance policy up to date?

Is it true that the safest place to be is in the center of God's will? What is the chapter and verse in the Bible for that one? Was Jonah safe when he walked around the enemy city for three days proclaiming God's judgment on them and their pending destruction? Radical obedience is a high risk venture.

Just ask
- Stephen, who was stoned to death,
- Paul, who was imprisoned,
- John the Baptist, who was beheaded,
- Jesus the Christ, Who was crucified.

If the safest place to be is in God's will, then is danger a sign that you are out of God's will? Hardly so! Some of the finest followers of Christ today live in the middle of daily danger and feel blessed to fellowship with Christ in His sufferings. Regardless of how highly Americans may value security, God is more into our surrender than our safety. He does not choose for us safety over significance.[13]

Neither does He choose polishing our image over procuring our obedience. In fact, when we obey God, we may appear crazy to others, as Jonah does when he marches into Nineveh with the breath of whale barf on him and seaweed still wrapped around his head. You might think, *If I'm going to obey the Lord, the least He can do for me is not make me look weird.* God doesn't work like that. Just ask Jesus: He was born in a barn! When we lose our desire to be acceptable in the eyes of man, then we are given a second chance to please God instead of man or self, and there is real joy.

Second chances in life often happen when we are willing to take risks. The surprising supernatural work of God begins when we give up being where *we* want to be and instead go where *God* wants us to be. We are so prone to choosing the path of least resistance that we never make it to our Nineveh, the dangerous place where God wants to use us in great ways. Take another chance and risk going wherever God would have you go.

Despite the danger, Jonah obediently begins walking around the huge city of the enemy. It was so large; Jonah walks for three days before he covers all the neighborhoods and business areas.

Imagine parking your car for three days and walking through every part of the city where you live. Would some areas of your city make you feel uncomfortable? Now imagine walking through every neighborhood of a middle-eastern capitol city shouting an unpopular message.

> On the day Jonah entered the city, he shouted to the crowds: "Forty days from now Nineveh will be destroyed!" (Jonah 3:4)

Speaking such brash, bold words, Jonah certainly does not expect to win a popularity contest! Obeying God and announcing that message could put Jonah in jail. However, Jonah remembers that disobeying God for the sake of one's own comfort often makes one very uncomfortable. So, on Jonah marches through the city, obediently doing what God said. As he marches and shouts, he is thankful that God has given him a second chance.

Is there something God has impressed on you to do recently, but you have not obeyed? What is it?

Do you truly believe that God is eager to give you a second chance? Will you take it?

Take a second chance at personal obedience to God.

Pray for a Second Chance for National Repentance

Jonah proclaims God's judgment on Nineveh, the capitol of an evil nation drunk with power and arrogance. With whale barf on his breath, Jonah shouts a one sentence sermon over and over again. To Jonah's surprise, that simple message results in an entire nation of proud people humbling themselves before God almighty.

> The people of Nineveh believed God's message, and from the greatest to the least, they decided to go without food and wear sackcloth to show their sorrow. (Jonah 3:5)

How odd of God to work in such a way. One day God has no fans in Nineveh, and three days later all the people of Nineveh are calling out to Him. Spiritual revival breaks out all across the nation of Assyria! Everywhere, people are bowing their knees in prayer, repenting before God. Who would have thought someone as unorthodox as Jonah could be used by God to bring about the repentance of a nation?

The renewal of a nation can happen through the most unlikely people and circumstances. Even now, fresh winds of the Spirit are beginning to blow in the United States. However, the winds are coming from unexpected people in previously unknown gatherings, and the new winds are not always welcome by institutionalized Christianity.

If America is to survive, we must turn back to God. If churches as we know them in America have become out of touch with the multitudes of people who need God, if our churches have become bored with the routine of handling the things of God, then don't be surprised if God brings radical people along to wake up America and upset the status quo of a sleeping church.

"Two thousand years ago, God started a revolt against the religion He started. So don't ever put it past God to cause a groundswell movement against churches and Christian institutions that bear His name … There is an uprising in the works and … no one less than God is behind it."[14]

When Jonah speaks God's message to Nineveh, hundreds of thousands of people repent and turn to God. This may be the greatest spiritual revival in history. Though there were no posters, no elegant preaching from famous orators, no coliseums filled to capacity, and no music sung, true revival breaks out across an entire city. Think of it! A one-sentence sermon brings a nation's capitol to its knees before God. This is not just any city; it is Nineveh, the most important city of the nation of Assyria, the most powerful nation on earth.

Look at how many second chances God gives in the Jonah story.

- In the midst of a deadly storm, the sailors turn from their idols to believe in the one true God, and the sea becomes calm.
- In the belly of a sea creature, when Jonah is finally ready to obey God, he finds himself spewed out onto dry ground.
- When the people of Nineveh turn from their sin, God changes His mind about destroying their nation.[15]

See the pattern in each instance? Man responds to God with a change of heart, and then God changes circumstances. If we are to live for God's glory rather than our own, we must experience brokenness over our own sin. First, we must let God's Spirit reveal to us our individual sin. We must let His spotlight examine every area of our lives. Then, we must confess to the Lord those areas of self-absorbed living. We must ask God to have mercy on us. Finally, we must challenge our entire nation to do the same.

Each of us as individuals needs a second chance at life. Nations who do not submit to God's leadership also need a second chance. What was wrong with Nineveh? Nineveh found her greatest security by building a strong national defense system and having more power than any other nation. The people of Nineveh were proud of their nation and their high standard of living.

Does that sound like a description of our own nation? Our nation as well is in need of another chance before God. May God give us another opportunity to become, once again, one nation under God. Why does America need to repent? What are the gods we serve? What's wrong with America?

Materialism has become the god of America. On Sunday mornings, our malls are more crowded than our churches. Because we are consumed with consumerism, we go deeper and deeper into debt and take the world down with us.

Individualism has left us thinking that God is a means to my ends. Americans are known as a people who are true to self. We must repent of "me first" living.

Humanism has made us believe that we are each a god of our own creation. We have fooled ourselves into thinking that we as humans have everything it takes to make a good life for ourselves.

Nationalism has caused us to believe that we as a nation are not only indivisible; we are also invincible and indestructible. If we get in trouble, all we need is a counter-terrorist force or a massive bail out.

Our nation's textbooks shame Hitler for killing millions of innocent people. They neglect to remind us of the unborn millions legally killed in our own land.

Morality has become too old fashioned for modern America. According to the Thomas Jefferson Research Institute, in the 1770s over 90 percent of our nation's educational thrust was aimed at teaching moral values. By 1926, the percentage of moral training had been reduced to 6 percent, and by 1951 the percentage was so low it could not even be measured.[16]

God is patient with nations. He could have destroyed Nineveh immediately, without giving them a forty-day eviction notice. However, God chooses to deal with them in the same merciful way he deals with us and with Jonah. Pray for God to give America a second chance before it is too late.

Ask yourself, "Am I burdened about the condition of our nation? What bothers me the most?"

Thank the Lord for a Second Chance at Heavenly Mercy

> When God saw that they had put a stop to their evil ways, He had mercy on them and didn't carry out the destruction He had threatened. (Jonah 3:10)

The people of Nineveh listen to Jonah and believe what he says. They deeply regret the way they have been cruel to other nations and know that they must seek God's forgiveness if they are to survive His wrath. The king decrees a nationwide season of prayer, fasting, and repentance. As a result, God decides not to destroy Nineveh.

God changes his mind, but He never changes His heart. His heart is set on pouring out compassion toward those who obey His will. When the people of Nineveh turn to God, God is free to release a blessing on them instead of a curse.

My problem is I don't understand the nature of God very well. I don't know Him intimately. If I were to really know Him, I would trust Him. The more I trust Him, the more risk I am willing to take for His sake. *God, cause my heart to fearlessly trust You.*

We hear of the judgment of God and assume that God is all about wrath. We picture God like a huge policeman in the sky, just waiting to catch us doing something wrong. However, judging man is not what gives God pleasure.

God is holy. Without something happening between imperfect man and perfect God, there can be no relationship. The result of man's self-absorbed living is separation from holy God. Separation is painful. It was so painful to God that He could not bear it any longer, so He Himself came to this earth to take the punishment for our sin. That's just how merciful He is.

What is God's mercy? It is His loving compassion for people and His tenderness of heart toward the needy.[17] Like a loving Father who hears and responds to the cry of his hurting child, even if the child was hurt while running away in rebellion, the Lord is deeply concerned about the pain of man.

Sometimes pain comes as a result of self-destructive disobedience. Such was the case with Jonah and with Nineveh. Even when you, through self-absorbed living, make a mess of your own life, God is ready and eager to extend mercy. God is merciful when He doesn't give you the consequences your disobedience deserves. Instead of doing away with you, He restores you, if you will only come to Him.

Maybe your God is too small. Because you are small, you can only imagine God to be a little better than the best person you know. Think of someone who has a big, kind heart. Chances are you can also think of a time when that same kind person's sudden inconsistency disappointed you. Even the most compassionate person can sometimes be uncaring.

The mercy of God is so consistent, it is beyond anything in your human experience. God is big enough to accept you regardless of what you have done. The Chinese character for "big" is written like this: 大. "Big" is one stroke short of "heaven," which is written like this: 天. Look at the character for "big" once again: 大. See the arms outstretched? God stands under heaven[18] with arms outstretched wide, ready to receive into His loving arms all who will return to Him. He stands before you today with open arms, ready for you to come back to Him. Run to Him!

Shannon needed another chance at life. She says, "I was confused when my dad left. I kept thinking, *It's not fair that you're not here for me. There you are spending time with your new family. I was here first.* I was lonely and hurting.

"Then when I was a senior in high school, I fell madly in love with this man. He was older, intelligent, owned this beautiful house, and he ran his own business. He had everything I ever wanted." Sometimes it's easier to believe in a love you can touch than a love that is real."[19]

"He was very controlling. I had to buy an entire new wardrobe because none of my clothes were good enough for him. He got mad at me so easily. One day he shoved me away from him."

"What I realized was that I was looking for attention in the same way that I looked for it from my father. I finally realized that I had been putting things first in my life that weren't worth putting first."

"I found myself calling out to God nightly, just begging for the pain to go away. I am in desperate need of Him. I need to know that I am loved. Christ brought me out of the pit. He raised me up. He's the one that can meet my needs from now on. He loves me, all the time, no matter what. He's there. He isn't distant. He's not going to shove me away. It's Him first. I am second."[20]

Shannon needed a second chance at love. She found that love in her Heavenly Father. Where in your life do you need God to give you a second chance?

Do you trust Him enough to let Him give you that second chance? Would you ask Him for it now?

How will you now live differently, having been given by God a second chance at life?

Is There Hope for America?

PEOPLE LOOKING FOR GOD SETTLED in America. They came looking for the freedom to worship Jesus. Is that an overstatement?

Rhode Island was chartered in 1683. These are the words of her charter: "We submit our persons, our lives, and our estates unto our Lord Jesus Christ, the King of Kings and the Lord of lords, and to all those perfect and absolute laws given us in His Holy Word."

The charter of Maryland says they were "formed by a pious zeal to extend the Christian Gospel." Delaware's charter says they were "formed for the further propagation of the Gospel of the Lord Jesus Christ." Connecticut's charter said their purpose was to "preserve the purity of the Gospel of the Lord Jesus Christ." [21]

There is perhaps no nation in the world that has been blessed in the unique ways that God has blessed America. We have great freedom in this land. For decades, we enjoyed the unusual security of not having our homeland attacked. Cars; airplanes; drinkable, running water; large air-conditioned dwellings; the certainty of rights being protected; and frequent dining out—all of these things make up the typical American way of life. However, to most people in the world, such a lifestyle is only an impossible dream.

We are very young as far as nations go. Will this nation, founded as "one nation under God," remain under Him? The United States is an experiment to see if a nation founded on trust in God can receive God's blessings yet still focus more on the "Blesser" than the blessings. While we have enjoyed unprecedented protection from enemies and a rich lifestyle unlike any other country's,[22] these very blessings may have resulted in our prideful thinking of ourselves as God's chosen nation and assuming we have arrived where we are today by our own human merit.

We once humbly credited the Lord God with all our blessings and successes. In earlier days of trials and losses, we turned to Him in utter dependence. What happened to the days when our men led their families to pray together, worship together, and grow in character together?

Now it's every man for himself, as self-indulgence, self-reliance, hyperindividualism, self-centeredness, and anti-family values are becoming the cultural norms of America. Now America attempts in vain to feel secure in our own strength. No wonder we feel so insecure these days. We think we are invincible and that God somehow cannot do without us, yet deep within we worry about our future. It's time for us to connect the dots between moral decay and national decline.

Perhaps the level of crime, calamities, domestic violence, terrorism, abortion, and corruption within the United States is a wake-up call from God. Each day our nation continues our claim to be "one nation under God," we are being given another gracious chance to actually become what we claim to be.

Yes, it's all right to ask God to bless America. However, it's more important that America blesses God. Let us use the blessings God has already showered on us to bless His name through living for His purposes instead of for own desires.

United States coins have always had the words "In God We Trust" imprinted on them. Take a look at the new one-dollar coin. Try to find those words. Where are they? It will take a microscope for you to see those words in tiny print on the thin outer edge of the coin.

We have pushed God to the margins of our lives, and it is reflected in our pushing Him to the very margins of our currency. We have edged God out from the center of our national being. These days nations rise and fall fairly rapidly. America is not immune to the possibility of collapse. History shows clearly what happens to nations that rely on their own strength instead of God. Whatever happened to the Roman Empire, which controlled the then-known world for hundreds of years? The U.S.S.R., which seemed to be such a stronghold of power, is now a thing of the past. Nations so easily come and go. Without God, we are not invincible; we are vulnerable.

Is there any hope for America? Our only hope is to bring Him to the center of our nation through national spiritual revival. America must genuinely turn back to God while we still have the chance. Our nation is broken down and in need of repair. If we are to be fixed, we must become spiritually broken before God.

Judgment on America is coming, and must be proclaimed. Be thankful that God is slow to anger. Each day that our nation does not self-destruct is one more chance God gives our nation to come back to Him.

What does it take for a nation to turn to God? First, there is a warning for us. Humans may follow a formula for repentance, yet God's judgment on a nation still may come. He is sovereign and will cause nations to rise and fall at His will. We can, however, learn from Nineveh the things that caused God to change His mind and give them a second chance. What must America do to have a future with God? Here's what is needed, according to Nineveh's experience, for a nation to become broken before God and get a second chance.

- The message of God is proclaimed.
- The people believe God's Word as truth.
- The people voluntarily fast to seek God.
- Grief over disobedience is expressed.
- Leaders of the nation humble themselves before God.
- Repentance becomes the heartbeat of the nation.
- There is earnest prayer to God.
- Specific national sins are confronted.
- Hope is placed in God's mercy.

Let's take a look at these one at a time.

The message of God must be proclaimed

> Then the Lord spoke to Jonah… "Deliver the message of judgment I have given you." (Jonah 3:1–2)

When the Word of God is boldly proclaimed to the people of a nation, that nation begins to have a hope for the future. Notice, however, that for national spiritual renewal to occur, the message needing to be proclaimed is not a feel-good message. Jonah's message wasn't one that would increase self-esteem. Before good news comes, people must be told in a straightforward way that there is sure judgment on sin.

What is it about Jonah's message that convinces the people of Nineveh? Had Jonah learned eloquent speech by enrolling in oratory classes? Was he well dressed? Did he have appealing credentials? Jonah had nothing but hard talk straight from God. He delivered a no-nonsense message. What gives the message power is that it is God's message. It is the truth. Power to convict and change the human heart comes from God's word, not merely our method of presentation.

America will rise or fall to the degree that God's people are willing to proclaim God's reaction to evils that persist on the national level. A person with abdominal pain may not enjoy hearing the news that he has a tumor needing removed by surgery. The message is hard but needed. The doctor needs to tell the person the truth, even though he or she may not want to hear it. Where are the Americans who will stand up for God today and tell His message of judgment on the sick sins of our nation?

What is the main reason that sin persists in our nation? Could it be that God's people have not boldly proclaimed sin to be sin? Are you afraid that if you speak up, people will not like you? Are you willing to become a voice proclaiming God's standard to people of our nation today?

The people must believe God's word as truth

> The people of Nineveh believed God's message. (Jonah 3:5)

Incredible! An unknown foreigner comes to town bringing with him a strange smell and an even stranger message, and instead of throwing him out of the city gates, the people believe what he says. Never underestimate the power of the Word of God to convict peoples' hearts.

If true, lasting revival is to sweep our nation, Americans must once again believe the Bible to be the completely reliable word of God. Believing in something is not just accepting the facts about it. It is acting accordingly. National repentance will begin when God's Word is clearly proclaimed and Americans respond by ordering their lives according to the priorities and commands in the Bible.

Many people today fear that the United States has no future. We are crumbling apart. Is there any hope? Some respond to this fear by placing hope in human attempts at rebuilding our nation. However, the Bible makes it clear that the future of our nation is not left to fate.

If our nation falls, it will not be because of the economy or terrorists. Nations most often fall not from external attacks, but from self-destruction. God allows a nation to rise or fall to the degree the nation humbly submits to His Word. Here's what He says:

> If I announce that a certain nation or kingdom is to be uprooted, torn down, and destroyed, but then that nation renounces its evil ways, I will not destroy it as I had planned.
>
> And if I announce that I will build up and plant a certain nation or kingdom, making it strong and great, but then that nation turns to evil

and refuses to obey me, I will not bless that nation as I had said I would. (Jeremiah 18:7-10)

Will America allow the word of God to once again define life for us? Will we return to the word of God? Do I allow the word of God to define life for me? Do I share the Word of God with others, encouraging them to live by the book?

People seek God by voluntarily fasting

> From the greatest to the least, they decided to go without food to show their sorrow. (Jonah 3:5)

Though they don't like what they hear, when the people of Nineveh receive the message from God spoken by Jonah, they know it has a definite ring of truth to it. They examine themselves and admit that they have followed their own ways. They have completely ignored the reality that God created them for His purposes.

In the moment of realizing this truth, the people of Nineveh see their own pride in personal accomplishments, their meanness to other people, and their disregard for God. Suddenly, arrogant self-reliance is replaced by embarrassment before God. They show their brokenness before God by going without food and water—fasting.

What is fasting? Fasting is voluntarily giving up food for spiritual purposes. Fasting is abstaining from eating in order to seek God.

When should we fast?[23] We should seek God instead of food when

- we need a heightened awareness of God,
- we need God's guidance,
- we are expressing grief,
- decisions need to be made,
- we are facing great temptation,
- we repent of sin.

Going without food has a way of refocusing us. When we fast, we find ourselves craving food at first. We think our bodies cannot go for an extended period of time without food. However, they can. To overcome the desire to eat, we need to turn to God for help with the craving. Soon

God reveals to us that we should be craving Him. A cleansing of the body, mind, and spirit occurs, resetting our beings to the Manufacturer's default: humble submission to our Creator God.

Throughout history, the people of God have fasted. During Biblical days, the people of God had an annual day of fasting. Believers around the world still fast to this day.

Many Koreans retreat alone to the mountains to pray and fast for days. I personally witnessed how some do so. The mountains of Korea are spiritual places. In the middle of winter, I visited a prayer mountain. The temperature was below zero. I saw men and women who were spending three days in uninterrupted fasting and praying. The amazing thing was how they folded their bodies into outdoor shelters the size of dog houses. There was no heat in these shelters. There was nothing but a light bulb for reading the Word of God. Wow! What desperate seeking of the Lord.

Is it any wonder that Korea is blessed with growing numbers of believers, with prosperity as a nation, and with the ability to enthusiastically send so many Koreans around the world as missionaries? God blesses countries who still seek Him through fasting.

We must become *desperate* for God in our lives and in our nation. Are you willing to take time out of your schedule to focus on God by fasting?

Should you fast? Though not commanded by God, fasting is an assumed, expected behavior of a follower of Christ. You should fast toward a spiritual purpose. Don't fast for the purpose of losing weight. If you cultivate the discipline of saying no to your body, you will be amazed at the power God will then give you to say no in other areas of your life. Go about life as normal, without calling attention to your fast. Don't order a t-shirt that says, "I'm fasting."

Get physically and spiritually prepared before you fast. Get good medical advice. On the front end, slowly reduce intake before the fast. During the fast, hunger will come. When the tummy reminds you it's time to eat, turn instead to the word of God, quiet time in solitude, helping those in need, prayer walking, or writing notes of encouragement to others.

Is God leading you to fast?[24] What needs to be spiritually addressed in your life through fasting?

Fasting is a voluntary means of people cleansing their hearts.

Deep grief over disobedience is expressed

> From the greatest to the least, they decided to … wear sackcloth to show their sorrow. (Jonah 3:5)

What happens when we are caught doing something wrong? Our typical human reaction is regret. However, that regret is usually simply remorse over getting caught. Being sorry about getting caught is not repentance at all, but merely self-centered shame for losing face. True repentance begins with expressing deep anguish that we have gone against what our Father desires. If we really love our Father, it will pain us to know we've disappointed Him.

The people of Nineveh hear the message from God, believe, and put on sackcloth. In those days, there was only one time when people would wear sackcloth, which is the equivalent of a potato sack. They dressed a dead person in sackcloth to prepare for burial.

When the people hear Jonah's message, they think they are as good as dead. They visualize their own funerals. They also cover themselves with dust and ashes. By putting dust on their heads, they express humility. They are also recognizing their own insignificance. They realize they came from dust and will return to dust. Dust on the head says that apart from God, man is insignificant. Putting dirt and ashes on your head reminds you of your own mortality, just as visualizing your own funeral does. Humble yourself before God. That's what the people of Nineveh were doing.

True repentance says, "God, we have ignored Your ways, and it hurts us so bad that we are as good dead. We'd rather die than go on like we have been. We feel such pain inside that we are dressing in the clothing of our own funerals."

To a truly repentant nation, the pain of seeing the nation in rebellion and sin is as great as the grief experienced over the death of a close family member. Let us grieve over the spiritual status quo of our nation at present.

What spiritual realities about America today cause you grief?

Though national repentance begins with a grassroots movement among everyday people, for it to truly touch the entire nation, people in national positions of great influence must experience a change of heart.

Leaders of the nation humble themselves before God.

> When the king of Nineveh heard what Jonah was saying, he stepped down from his throne and took off his royal robes. (Jonah 3:6)

Who is this king? He is Assur Dan III.[25] Nineveh is the key city of the nation of Assyria. Had Nineveh not experienced national revival because of the preaching of Jonah, it would have been destroyed. Instead, Nineveh turns to God and is soon blessed with influence in becoming the nation's capitol.

During the time leading up to Jonah's message, Assyria experienced earthquake, famine, rioting, and war. Surely all these things inclined King Assur Dan III to listen to what God was saying through this most unusual prophet.

Look again at what this great king does. He steps down from his high throne. All eyes are on him. The people surely turn to each other and ask, "Why has he made himself low by stepping down from his lofty throne? What will he say or do next?" They watch as he does something they've never seen before. The king takes off his royal robe. A gasp is heard among the people. What happens next?

> He dressed himself in sackcloth and sat on a heap of ashes. (Jonah 3:6)

Here we have one of the most powerful kings of history stripping himself of his royal robe in public, dressing in old potato sacks, and sitting on a heap of ashes. Many kings are known in history books by how many people died for them or how many lands they conquered. However, this king is known for something far greater: humbling himself before God Almighty.

True revival occurs when the leaders of the nation put away their personal image polishing, openly mourn over the spiritual state of the nation, and repent of national and personal arrogance.

Leadership guru Ken Blanchard was invited to the White House by former president Bill Clinton. Several pastors who advised the president were present at the dinner. Blanchard asked Clinton who he looked to as his leadership model. Without hesitating, Clinton said, "John F. Kennedy."

Blanchard remarked that we tend to become like those we look to as models. He then asked the president, "Have you ever considered Jesus as a leadership role model?" The president replied that he had not.

Blanchard turned to the pastors at the dinner and said, "Let's stop and think how these years in the president's office would have turned out differently had someone challenged the president to lead like Jesus." The room became quiet.

Pray that the leaders of America would come down from their thrones, take off their royal robes, and humble themselves before Almighty God.

What is your personal prayer for our nation's leaders?

When our leaders look to the Lord for leadership, the nation will turn back to God. Then what happens?

Repentance becomes the heart cry of our nation.

> And he issued a proclamation and it said, "In Nineveh by the decree of the king and his nobles: Do not let man, beast, herd, or flock taste a thing. Do not let them eat or drink water. But both man and beast must be covered with sackcloth." (Jonah 3:7–8 NASV)

Jonah shouts, "Repent!" That's exactly what needs to happen. We must become deeply disturbed and convicted about who we are on the inside. Our sense of self must be challenged.

The king told the people to express sincere humiliation before holy God in two ways: every person and every animal was to fast and wear sackcloth. What an unusual decree from the commander in chief of a nation. Animals that are not fed on schedule become very irritable and begin braying and bawling. What a ruckus repentance creates!

Can you imagine the president of our nation announcing that all the people of America are to spend a day in prayer and fast before God for the sake of our nation? As strange as it sounds, that is exactly what several American presidents have done in the past.

On occasion, our presidents have called on the entire nation to spend an entire day in prayer and fasting. John Adams called for a national day of prayer and fasting in 1798. James Madison did the same during his time as president. Three times while he was president during the Civil War, Abraham Lincoln called on the entire nation to spend a day humbly before God in prayer and fasting.

Archeologists have discovered that the people of Nineveh lived in great luxury. They wore beautiful garments adorned with fine gems. However, when true repentance grips their hearts, they exchange their fancy garments for the ultimate expression of deep pain and grief: goat-hair sacks usually worn only by a corpse at a funeral.

True repentance is a change of heart, not merely fasting then going right back to the same behavior. The repentant heart has a change of values. However, true repentance is also a change of lifestyle.

Imagine in one decree from the president, all individual fashion statements are banned. A humiliating uniform is mandated as the only thing allowed to be worn by anyone. Why would Assur Dan make such a decree? These uniforms and the accompanying fast are constant lifestyle reminders of heartfelt repentance before God. What changes should our nation make to demonstrate our desperation for God?

In Nineveh we have an entire nation of people ignoring God, living in indulgent self-absorption, and being cruel to their enemies. Could God possibly forgive them? Certainly! However, the nation must truly repent. The only time God holds our behavior against us is when we refuse to repent. When repentance becomes a national agenda, the heart of the nation begins to beat as one with God's heart. What would it take for repentance to become the heart cry of the United States?

What leads to national revival?

Earnest prayer is brought before God.

> Everyone is to ... pray earnestly to God. (Jonah 3:8)

King Assur Dan III of Nineveh makes a clear statement about whether or not it is politically correct to pray in public. He says it is not just allowable—it is to be expected. If America is to turn to God, prayer must once again become a vital part of who we are as a nation.

What difference can prayer make in a nation? On September 23, 1857, a businessman named Jeremiah Lamphier called on American businessmen to pray for the violence, crime, poverty, the collapse of families and racial hatred in America to stop. Our country was in such a sad state that many wondered if America was possibly writing the last chapter of its history.

Businessmen closed their shops during lunch and gathered to pray for the nation they loved. Many men turned to the Lord during these prayer meetings. Families committed to staying together. Divine fire broke out across America. Even entire crews of vessels traveling to America, on hearing of the revival, became deeply convicted of sin even before arriving in America.

As a result of the businessmen's noon prayer meetings, conservative estimates claim that more than a million people met Jesus Christ as Savior in less than a twelve-month span.[26] God, do it again!

Pray for specific sins of our nation. Though we may not have personally participated in the sin, we should still confess those national sins before God and repent of them. Modern culture would have us believe we are no longer our brother's keeper, but the Bible shows us clearly that we are. We must hold each other and our nation accountable for moral choices. Here's a prayer for our nation and its leaders.

> Heavenly Father, we come before you today to ask Your forgiveness and to seek Your direction and guidance.
>
> We know Your Word says, "Woe to those who call evil good," but that is exactly what we have done. We have lost our spiritual equilibrium and reversed our values.
>
> We confess that we have *ridiculed the absolute truth of Your Word* and called it *Pluralism*;
>
> We have *worshipped other gods* and called it *multiculturalism*;
>
> We have *endorsed perversion* and called it *alternative lifestyle*;
>
> We have *exploited the poor* and called it the *lottery*;
>
> We have *rewarded laziness* and called it *welfare*;
>
> We have *killed our unborn* and called it *choice*;
>
> We have *shot abortionists* and called it *justifiable*;

We have *neglected to discipline our children* and called it *building self esteem*;

We have *abused power* and called it *politics*;

We have *coveted our neighbor's possessions* and called it *ambition*;

We have *polluted the air with profanity and pornography* and called it *freedom of expression*;

We have *ridiculed the time-honored values of our forefathers* and called it *enlightenment*.

Search us, Oh, God, and know our hearts today; cleanse us from every sin and set us free.

Guide and bless these men and women who have been sent to direct us to the center of Your will.

We ask these things in the name of Your Son, the living Savior, Jesus Christ. Amen.[27]

Prayer for national repentance has been known to lead to dramatic spiritual breakthroughs for an entire country. Our nation seems far removed from the commandments of the Lord. God is looking for people who will stand in the gap, praying vicariously for the disobedience of our nation.

Write a prayer for our nation:

_____
_____
_____

Is there hope for America? To be fixed, we must realize we are broken down. We must come before God with broken hearts over our sin. What happens in order for a nation to get a second chance with God?

Specific national moral issues are addressed.

> Everyone must turn from their evil ways and stop all their violence. (Jonah 3:9)

Previously only concerned about expanding the country's power through violence, the King of Nineveh suddenly becomes much more concerned about the moral condition of the country. He decrees that everyone must take a long look at their behavior and stop doing things that are wrong.

The country had been deceiving itself into believing that there were no moral absolutes. Now faced with the consequences of such free thinking, the king says in effect, "We must own up to our own actions. We have sinned. Now we must stop doing so, seek God, and follow His standard of right and wrong once again."

Some who hear King Assur Dan's words think, "He's not talking to me. I've never done anything terribly bad. I don't have anything to repent about."

There is such a thing as corporate guilt. To be a member of a society that overlooks moral compromise is to be a part of the guilt and the consequences such a society must face. Corporate guilt requires corporate confession of the nation's sin.[28]

Crime is increasing so fast that we are unable to build prisons fast enough to house the offenders. If America is to turn back to God, issues such as debt, pornography, violence, theft, murder, abortion, sexual perversion, laziness, gluttony, and immorality must be addressed on the national level.

Some Christians today use political or secular means such as lobbying, boycotting, and protesting to advance their values. However, if there is to be a genuine renewal of our nation, it will come about not by physical but by *spiritual* means such as prayer, fasting, and repentance. When we are genuinely seeking God as a nation, then right and wrong will become a great concern to society. Without God's mercy, a nation who ignores Godly values has no hope.

Hope is placed in God's mercy

> "Who can tell? Perhaps even yet God will have pity on us and hold back his fierce anger from destroying us." (Jonah 3:9)

Literally, the verse says, "The people *turned* from evil and said, 'Maybe God will *turn* from His decree.'"

Imagine that you are Jonah and you have just spent three days walking the city telling people there was no hope for them because God would soon destroy their city. You believe God will do just that. Then you see an unexpected reaction from the people. They dress in sackcloth, get on their knees, and pray in sincere repentance. That's what happened to Jonah. He must have been totally stunned.

"Who knows? Maybe God will change his mind," the king says.

Jonah may have laughed and sarcastically responded, "Yeah, sure! Don't you know that you are dealing with the Creator of the universe, Who is steadfast and immovable? Where in the world do you get the idea that God might possibly change His mind on what He has decreed?"

Perhaps the king got the idea from Jonah. The king likely heard the story of how God had given Jonah a second chance by miraculously sending a big fish to save Jonah's life. God gave Jonah a second chance; maybe, he would give Nineveh another chance as well.

Our only hope is to desperately come before God, admitting to Him that we are broken down. What if our nation turned to God as Nineveh did? What would be the modern day equivalent of fasting, putting on sackcloth, sprinkling ashes on the head, and turning from evil? What would such repentance look like in modern America?

Welcome to My Pity Party!

HERE I SIT IN A waiting room at the Mayo Clinic in Rochester, Minnesota. The news from the doctor is not good. Recently when we were living in Hong Kong, my wife, Cheryl, was diagnosed with a brain tumor. Radiation was performed on the tumor almost immediately. The doctor says it may take several more years before the radiation might cause the tumor to shrink. We are slowly accepting the reality that our lives will never be as they were before. To be honest, there are times when I want to have a pity party.

The party would start off with a series of announcements.

"Ladies, and Gentlemen, you have gathered here today to confirm how pitiful I am. Consider the following:

- Did you know that the air conditioner went out in my car?
- My arms are not long enough to hold the book in focus.
- There are more weeds in our yard than I can pull.
- Someone ate my favorite ice cream out of the fridge without my permission.
- I stubbed my toe in the dark.
- Did I mention that my wife Cheryl has a brain tumor? Poor, pitiful Matthew! Welcome to my pity party."

What qualifies a person to have a pity party? Cheryl is surely more entitled than me, especially if her husband is insensitive and self-centered, yet she has no plans at all for such a party. Just how bad do things have to get before we can say, "Now that person *deserves* to have some self-pity"?

When you wake up in the morning, do you rise and shine, or do you rise and whine? Some people rise and whine, like Winnie the Pooh does sometimes. Though the cuddly Pooh Bear seems happy most of the time, he has his moments of occasional self-pity. Do you wake up saying something you might expect Winnie the Pooh to say?

"Oh bother, here I am just a bear of little brains in this unfair world. My life is surely worse than that of *all* the other creatures in the forest.

They are all out having fun, and here I am with my head stuck in the honey jar. There's not much to be done for the fix I'm in. Oh, bother! Welcome to my pity party!"

Self-pity occurs when your response to adverse situations is to mope or just eat lots of honey, like Pooh does. Merely another form of self-absorption, self-pity causes you to believe you are the victim of events, deserving of sympathy. It is a means of self-soothing or self-nurturing. Feeling sorry for self is one way of refusing to take responsibility. The Pooh Bear in each of us loves to throw a party so friends can hear about our latest misery.

We each respond differently to the challenges of life. Some people don't let anything knock the wind out of their sails. Others get a pimple on their nose and think that the whole world is quickly coming to an end. Drama queens and kings see in every situation an opportunity to overreact.

What's the difference? Some people, after merely getting a flat tire, can spin into a downward cycle of depression. Other people are diagnosed with cancer, yet rise above it to experience surprising opportunities hidden within life's difficulties. Why is this so? *The difference, in part, is in whether or not we succumb to self-pity.*

Condoleezza Rice had every reason to become a nobody. She grew up in the South during a time of severe prejudice. Storeowners refused to allow her to buy clothes. There were certain restaurants where "her kind" was not allowed. Despite her exceptional academic record, she was told that she simply was not university material. Yet Rice has become one of the most internationally respected leaders of the United States of America. Rice says, "Struggle and sorrow are not a license to give way to … self-pity."[29]

When does self-pity come your way?

The answer may be surprising. Self-pity doesn't necessarily come from losing a job or going through a divorce. It can come through the smallest, silliest things. A bad hair day can cause someone to sulk and avoid spending time with people. A cutting remark made by a friend can cause a person to go home and pout the rest of the day.

The root cause of pity is not the bad hair or the comment made by a friend. *Self-pity is not caused by what happens to you. It's caused by what happens to what happens to you.* Your response to your situation is more important than the situation itself.

Let's look at how two frogs handle a sticky situation. One frog accidentally jumps into a bucket of milk and soon drowns because there is no way out. Another frog jumps into the same bucket, and swims and kicks so much that he churns the milk into butter, then hops right out. Do you drown in self-pity? Instead, take your difficult situation and do something about it. Start churning butter!

Jonah is the perfect case study on self-pity. He's the frog that drowned in a deep bucket of his own pitiful tears. Let's dissect that frog and discover from Jonah four causes for self-pity. Here's the first way that self-pity comes about.

Self-pity comes when God doesn't follow your agenda.

Jonah reluctantly obeys God, goes to Nineveh, and tells the people there that God is going to destroy their city in forty days. He is sure God will do just that. Guess what? Despite our attempts at putting God in a box, He tends to jump out. If we think we understand the ways of God and know His next move, we have another think coming.

God is not obligated to follow Jonah's agenda, and He is not obligated to follow yours. When God sees the people of Nineveh genuinely repenting and turning to Him, God changes His mind[30] and does not destroy Nineveh. How does Jonah respond to this change of plans?

> This change of plans upset Jonah, and he became very angry. (Jonah 4:1)

The sovereignty of God is, to Jonah, an upsetting reality. Jonah wants things to turn out the way he has them planned in his own mind. He visualizes the future and then snaps his fingers to bring it about. However, Jonah finds there is no omnipotent power within his fingertips.

Jonah is under the delusion that he is in charge of his own destiny and the destiny of others. A primary cause of the anger of self-pity is the delusion that we are in control of circumstances. To think we control circumstances is merely another way of saying we think we are in control of God. When God doesn't follow our agenda, we feel entitled to a pity party.

Do you see yourself as the one in charge of your own destiny? If you do, you'll get angry toward God and start seeking pity from others. You will always find people willing to give it to you.

Jonah has a hissy fit. "He became very angry," Jonah 4:1 says. The word used in the Bible to describe Jonah is the Hebrew word that means "really upset and totally ticked off." You can just see his face getting red and the steam rising from the top of his head.

One of my seventh-grade teachers was in her first year of teaching, and she would easily lose control of the class, then become raging mad. When she got into her fury, it seemed like steam would come out of her so fast it caused her hair to frizz up before the students' eyes. That's how she earned the nickname "Ms. Frizz." When the Bible says that Jonah is fuming mad, I have a mental picture of what that looks like.

What is the primary reason that we become angry and disappointed with God? Because He has not considered us as equal partners in the decision-making process. That, my friend, is the issue. We get angry because we are not equal partners with God.

When we, like Jonah, are more committed to our concept of how God should act than we are committed to who God is, we set ourselves up for serious frustration.

When God changes my circumstances without first consulting me, I get ticked off. There I go pouting, angry at God for acting so big and powerful. "God, You're only supposed to ride shotgun beside me through life, like my co-pilot. I'll call You whenever I need You. Just who do You think You are taking over the wheel? Have You forgotten that I am the captain of my own ship?"

If you are wallowing in self-pity, you may be confused about who is responsible for what. Our culture says you are responsible for your own destiny, and spirituality is there to help you fulfill your dreams. No wonder so many people today have become fatalistic. When we chase our own dreams, we pity ourselves for not finding the pot at the end of the rainbow. When we allow God to reveal His dreams for us, we are surprised to find how big and exciting His dreams are.

Are you expecting God to follow *your* agenda? Or do you seek to follow *His* agenda for you? Self-pity comes when God does not follow your agenda. When else does it come?

Self-pity comes when your character falls way short of God's nature.

Jonah is upset that God changed His mind. Let's see what Jonah does next.

> So he complained to the Lord about it: "Didn't I say before I left home that You would do this, Lord? That is why I ran to Tarshish! I knew that You were a gracious and compassionate God, slow to get angry and filled with unfailing love. I knew how easily You could cancel Your plans for destroying these people." (Jonah 4:2)

Jonah justifies his own prior rebellion. "God, I told You so!" he whines. "Didn't I tell You before I left home that if I went to Nineveh and preached judgment, they might repent and You might change Your mind about destroying them? I know you are the God of love, but love has its limits."

Jonah continues, "We've had this conversation once already, God. Do you still not get it? Read my lips: *I don't like these people!* Now I don't like *You* either, because You like *them*! You are on *their* side, not mine! I wish I'd kept running from You instead of coming here and seeing *this* happen! God, there are some people you're just not supposed to love."

When God looks favorably on those we consider undeserving of His favor, we are not always happy. Sometimes we mope in self-pity. We forget that none of us deserves His favor.

Self-pity leads a person to some insane conclusions. "God, you are responsible for my misery. If You would only be more like me, God, then I'd be happy!" The whiner has deceived himself into some very twisted ways of thinking.

When who you are isn't getting closer to who God wants you to be, there is a storm at heart. Though God rescued Jonah from the storm at sea, and though outwardly Jonah obeys God by going to Nineveh, Jonah is still a rebel at heart. He refuses to see other people with God's compassion. At the heart of Jonah's self-pity is a very serious character flaw: he cares about no one but himself.

God's mercy bothers Jonah. God's heart and Jonah's heart aren't beating as one.

While we criticize Jonah, we ourselves are guilty. Oh, we love to sing "Amazing Grace," but then we want to decide who gets it. It's not easy to be happy when God gives His grace freely to those who we feel don't deserve it.

What if the quiet neighborhood you live in were to become a mixture of many ethnic groups, described by neighbors as undesirable people who lower the value of property? Would you join in on the pity party, or would you do as one north Dallas couple does? This couple receives great joy from using their home, now in a transitional community, to teach many of their new neighbors English and other life skills.

What if sketchy people from the dark side of town were to believe in the Lord and become a part of the new-member classes in your church? Would you be hesitant to accept repentant thieves, murderers, drug-dealers, and hookers as new brothers and sisters in Christ?

If a group of Middle Eastern business men in your city began coming to your men's prayer breakfast and started asking startling but sincere questions about your faith, would the church leadership be happy for the opportunity or would they beef up security in the building?

Let's define character. Character is determined by how you react to your circumstances. Character is who you are when no one is looking. Self-pity leads you to think you are not responsible for your own character development. When someone challenges your character flaws, you say, "I am who I am. No one is going to tell me how to think or what to do." Do you really want to go through the rest of your life stagnant, just as you are now?

As Jonah goes to Nineveh, he appears to have a change of heart. He is physically going where God said to go, but his obedience is not from the heart. Just like Jonah, we often mask a heart of rebellion with external actions that give us an obedient appearance. Then when no one is looking, we do whatever it takes to get what we want. Character is who you are in private when no one is looking. Reputation is what others *think* you are. In a choice between character and reputation, which are you more concerned about? May God grant you both, with a priority on character!

The self-pity in me is coupled with pride, which keeps me appearing religious for the sake of my own glory. I never grow in maturity this way.

If we haven't developed in character, we can't cope when crisis comes. Sooner or later, circumstances inevitably put us in a squeeze and our character deficiency oozes out. Our cover is blown!

So many problems today arise from the self-centered immaturity of people who have the mere appearance of obedience to God. *Appearing* to be obedient and *being* obedient are entirely different things.

When you obey God, do you do so because you feel you have to keep God happy? You don't want to live in the belly of a fish, so the Jonah in you obeys God. If you obey God because the alternative is not very appealing, that is shallow obedience. If you obey God because you feel you must, you may still have a rebellious heart.[31] It's hard to keep being obedient if you are obeying for selfish reasons. Joyful, lasting obedience only comes from a heart genuinely surrendered to God's sovereignty.

Self-pity comes when God doesn't follow your agenda, and that makes you angry. Pity also comes when your character falls way short of God's nature, which results in rebellion. There's more.

Self-pity comes when there's nothing more to life than self.

In his crazed state of telling God off, Jonah has lost all sense of perspective on the situation. Jonah is overreacting so severely that a bystander watching Jonah's temper tantrum would laugh at Jonah, thinking he is surely practicing a role in a dramatic production. If the bystander were a radio reporter live at the scene, here is what he might say.

"I'm standing here this afternoon outside Nineveh. There is a rather strange man who smells like … whale barf! He is apparently named Jonah. Right now, he is jumping up and down with arms flailing and fists swinging. Shouting at God, Jonah is going stark raving mad over God's kindness to these people of Nineveh."

"Although Jonah is supposed to be representing God, he is instead acting like a spoiled brat, making threats to run away from home if he doesn't get his way. Rather humorous, actually. Jonah sees his situation as so terrible—he just wants God to end his life. Let's listen in to hear what Jonah is saying to God."

> Just kill me now, Lord! I'd rather be dead than alive. (Jonah 4:3)

The radio reporter brings the microphone closer to Jonah's mouth, who says, "God, if you are not going to kill them like I think you should, then just kill me! My life is as good as over anyway. You have caused me to lose all credibility! I can't imagine how I could become more pitiful than this!"

Jonah is behaving like a teenager, that adolescent stage of life which tends to be me-centered. The sad truth is that many adults never grow up on the inside. Many people who are forty, sixty, and even eighty years old are still stuck with a teenage worldview.

Even though we know better, we insanely still believe that the whole world exists to make us happy. Where has this idea come from? Well, we were all born with a nature that puts self first. To top it off, our American way of living reinforces this idea. In our self-absorbed world today, is it any wonder there are so many pitiful, depressed people?

Self-pity comes from thinking more about self than we should. Even answering all the introspective questions within the pages of this book could lead you as the reader to feel sorrow for yourself. So make this book a quick read, and then get on with selfless living. Though an occasional thought of pity for self can serve to snap us out of introspection and redirect us toward serving God and others, there is no good result from lingering in pity.

When you finally begin to realize you are not the center of the universe and the world just isn't *ever* going to revolve around you, you get mad at God and ask Him to stop the world and let you get off this not-so-merry-go-round of life. Pity actually creates a pitiful reality. You see things as worse than they actually are. Just ask suicidal Jonah. Self-pity can result in depression so dark that the end of life is desired. Depression doesn't just affect *you*; it affects your family and friends. Suicide is a cop-out. It has devastating effects on family and friends.

You were not created to live for self. You see, when self becomes your primary reason for existence in this world, what you actually experience is far different than what you expect.

- You set self up for continual frustration.
- You are repeatedly surprised that life isn't fair.
- You search in vain for the genie in a bottle that can magically bring you personal fulfillment.

When things don't happen the way you planned, you conclude that you are just not trying hard enough. On you go in search of meaning in life by looking nowhere but in the mirror. You must polish your image. However, your highly protected profile just keeps getting tarnished. Now you can't even clearly see the image through all your tears. Self-pity comes when there's nothing more to life than self, and the result is depression.

There is one final thing that can bring self-pity.

Self-pity comes when your picture of a perfect future just isn't happening

Jonah is embarrassed. He has spoken with such firm conviction on how Nineveh's days are numbered. He thought he was the final voice of authority on the subject. Declaring doom and gloom brings Jonah great pride and satisfaction, but now he must eat his words. Self-absorption leads the Jonah in us to a depressing point where our primary life goal is to enhance our own image. Jonah has lost so much face that he wants to die.

> I'd rather be dead than alive because nothing I predicted is going to happen. (Jonah 4:3)

Jonah feels God is making him look bad. Because of what God has done, Jonah has lost face.

When I speak with certainty that some event will come about, only to see something completely different happen, I am embarrassed. I have held myself up as a great authority, but now other people know that I too, am just a mere mortal. How humiliating! I've lost face. I promised one thing would happen, but the exact opposite has happened. I can never show my face in public again.

How awful, though, that Jonah cares more about being right than he does about the salvation of a nation. Self-centeredness distorts our thinking.

Self-pity comes from the pride of thinking we can predict our own future. For the prideful person making predictions with absolute certainty, self-pity waits just around the corner. Self-pity comes when my predicted future just isn't happening. The result is loss of face.

Let's take a look at a summary of self-pity.

Self-pity comes when…	Self-pity results in…
God doesn't follow my agenda	Anger
My character falls way short of God's nature	Rebellion
There's nothing more to life than me	Depression
My predicted future just isn't happening	Loss of Face

Of the four causes of self-pity on the left, which one is the most problematic for you?

Take another look at the right side of the chart. Are any of these results of self-pity evident in your life?

It's not enough just to know what causes self-pity. The tendency to pout over circumstances is a natural human response that doesn't go away just by recognizing it. Unless there is outside intervention like Pooh received from Christopher Robin, our heads will still be stuck in the honey jar. It's crucial that you know how to deal with self-pity. Is there anyone bigger and smarter than us who can help us with our pity? Someone like, maybe, God? Here's a key question:

Is it all right to invite God to your pity party?

Should you invite God to your pity party? Perhaps your initial human reaction is that you dare not do so. You want to hide your true self from God. You don't want the embarrassment of showing your ugly side to God. God might get mad at you!

When Jonah has his pity party and God comes as the not-so-honored guest, how does it turn out? Does God shower His wrath down on Jonah? When Jonah has his little temper tantrum, does God bend Jonah over His knee and spank him?

> The Lord replied, "Is it right for you to be angry about this?" (Jonah 4:4)

God patiently tries to bring delusional Jonah back to a sane way of thinking. Jonah refuses to listen, and instead goes off on yet another temper tantrum. God patiently asks Jonah a second time the very same question. "Is it right for you to be so upset, Jonah?" God does not mind Jonah telling Him how he feels. In fact, it seems God has actually been waiting for this frank talk with Jonah.

Listen, God is big enough to handle whatever emotional crises we work ourselves into. There is nothing we can tell Him that will surprise Him. Yes, it's all right to invite God to an embarrassing display of pouting. In fact, it is mandatory. To withhold negative emotions is to deny God entrance into the deepest chambers of our hearts.[32] But we do this so often. We keep from Him the ugly parts of us that are in the most need of His healing.

Are you tired of doing that? I'm now holding up my right hand and asking you as the reader to do the same. Make a risky vow with me. Please repeat after me.

> I promise (I promise)
> to invite God (to invite God)
> to my next (to my next)
> pity party (pity party).

Now, don't you feel better already? Hiding our pity from God keeps us from experiencing God's presence. Transparency brings us into His arms. When is the best time to invite God to your party? When should He arrive? He should be the very first one to arrive, so you should invite Him to come a little earlier than your friends. Many times we turn to friends before we talk to God. It should be the other way around. Well-meaning friends can sometimes actually reinforce our idea that we are pitiful. However, God is not like that. He will patiently listen to us and then seek to rearrange our hearts to bring emotional healing.

Don't wait to express your emotions to God until you are like Jonah—at the point of a volcanic eruption of anger. By then, chances are you are in no condition to allow God to teach you *anything* through the situation.

The time to share your emotions with God is earlier, not later. You should regularly keep Him tuned in to your emotions instead of blocking Him out until you are at the point of making threats against Him.

We must not refuse to admit before God that we are dealing with self-pity. Sometimes we feel that we must show others and God how emotionally on top of things we are. We think we are supposed to have our act together. Sometimes we refuse to admit that we don't. We forget, though, that God is big enough to handle our problems and is the best confidant.

If you have a pity party and don't invite God, you experience two negative results:

- First, you waste an important opportunity for God to give you a new frame of mind. God's new perspective can give you wings to soar like an eagle over your challenges and help you grow strong through your circumstances.
- Second, you end up inviting other people, and they just show pity for you. Don't misunderstand. Friends are a key resource in overcoming self-pity; however, rare is the friend who challenges you to quit being self-absorbed. Many times your friends are afraid to say, "Snap out of it," because they are afraid of how you will take it. They are afraid you won't appreciate the honesty.

Friends do not have the patience and wisdom of God in helping bring about change. In fact, they may join you in feeling sorry for you, reinforcing your idea that you are a helpless victim of circumstances. Though they may provide some comfort, friends alone cannot pull you out of your quandary without God showing up at your pity party.

Jonah is right in expressing his emotions to God, even if he isn't thinking straight. That's exactly when God needs to straighten out our thinking. He can handle honest sharing of feelings. We must not worry about emotionally scarring Him. He is a patient, understanding, and loving Father.

So feel free to invite Him to your next pity party. Yes, it really is all right to do so! Just come to Him with a true, heartfelt desire to share your emotions with Him just as you are here and now, and then ask Him to help you see your situation from His perspective. If you are to overcome pity, you must be open to share your true feelings with God, and then accept God's perspective on your situation.

Now here's the bottom-line question:

What should be done with self-pity?

It's not enough to admit we have a problem with pity. We need to know what to do with that pouting, withdrawal, and anger that results from self-pity. From Jonah's bad example, we learn four good lessons. Here's how to handle self-pity.

See God at work in your circumstances

What Jonah sees as a huge problem is actually an incredible victory. God uses Jonah to bring about the revival of an entire nation of people. Jonah should be overjoyed!

Cheryl and I served as missionaries for twenty years in East Asia during a time of great spiritual harvest. We often saw groups of people turn to Christ. Helping start new churches was a regular event for us. Many of our friends, however, went to more difficult mission fields where missionaries would rejoice if even one person were to follow Christ.

Jonah was sent by God to just such a difficult mission field in the Middle East. In such challenging places, any missionary in his right mind would love to report that an entire city has repented and turned to God. However, Jonah is not in his right mind. He cannot be happy with God using him to impact an entire city. Self-pity gets us out of our right minds and blinds us so we cannot see the hand of God at work in our current circumstances.

Learn to look beyond what you think of as a difficulty to see what God is doing in your life. He is actively at work in your situation bringing His favor on you. Look for the victory He's already accomplishing through you. God works for the good of those who love Him and who are called according to His purpose.

If Jonah would realize the great victory unfolding before his eyes in Nineveh, he would *not* go away from the city by himself to have a pity party. Instead, Jonah would remain in the city to celebrate the salvation of an entire nation. [33] His pity party causes him to miss out on a better and happier party. Your pity may cause you to miss out on life's celebrations.

When you look at your circumstances and don't like what you see, you need to ask God for some new glasses. Learn to look at your circumstances from a different angle. Then when you see God at work through your trials, anger toward God is replaced with the joy of the Lord. Give up the tiresome life of a self-centered pessimist. Choose to live as a God-centered optimist. What good things is God already doing in your situation?

Some friends asked me if I feared that my wife's recently diagnosed brain tumor might affect our ministry in the future. I replied, "The tumor has most definitely *already* affected our ministry. Cheryl's brain tumor has made us more compassionate to hurting people, more concerned about meeting each other's needs, and more dependent on God. However, none of those things are things to fear."

See God at work doing good things in your current circumstances and the joy of the Lord will flood your life. Who wants to live life devoid of joy?

Back to our question: what should you do with self-pity?

Let trials build character in you

Dr. Sinclair B. Ferguson says, "When we respond to trials as a means of character development, we are investing in our future usefulness."[34] Trials by fire burn away our impurities, and what's left is solid gold character. How can we prove our character if no challenges ever come? Through fellowship with Christ in dark days, His presence guides us to be more like Him.

How can we make sense out of suffering? Paralyzed from the neck down after a diving accident, Joni Erickson Tada's life changed forever. As a teenager at a camp run by Young Life, Joni understood the Gospel and gave her life to Christ. Just before her accident, she prayed, "Lord if you're really there, do something in my life to change me around. I'm begging you!"

After weeks in a special frame for her body, she began rehab and physical therapy at a nursing home. During this time she battled with depression and self-pity. She wanted to commit suicide. Her faith was severely tested. This drove her to the Bible.

Now Joni sings, draws with her mouth, speaks in public, cares for children, writes and ministers to disabled people, and uses her radio program to distribute wheelchairs around the world. Joni says, "Only God knows why I was paralyzed. Maybe He knew I'd be ultimately happier serving Him. If I were still on my feet, it's hard to say how things would have gone. I probably would have drifted through life …"

Through Joni's trials, God is doing incredible things by changing the lives of thousands of people. Remember, it's not about what happens to you, but your response to what happens to you. Joni responded to her circumstances by allowing the Lord to change who she was from the inside out. Trials are allowed by God to give us deeper fellowship with Christ in His suffering.

Be done with self-absorbed living

George Barna, author of *Think Like Jesus*, challenges believers to make our thought life more like Jesus'. "The more you can purge yourself of you, and replace it with a wholehearted focus on and surrendering of self to God, the more fulfilling your life will be,"[35] Barna said.

I must stop believing this world was created to serve me. I was created to serve God and others. I must believe that and start acting on my belief. Serving others makes me happy.

"When I was in high school, I reacted to life selfishly and never built on any long-lasting values, and almost always at the expense of others," Joni said.

"But now you're happy?" a teenage girl asked.

"I really am. I wouldn't change my life for anything. I feel privileged. I'm really thankful He did something to get my attention and change me. You know, you don't have to get a broken neck to be drawn to God. I hope you'll learn from my experience and not have to go through the bitter lessons of suffering that I had to face in order to learn."[36]

When you are no longer absorbed in self, pity has nothing to grab hold of. In selfless living, pity cannot take hold of you. With self taken out of the spotlight, God takes center stage in your life, and you gain His perspective.

Hold on loosely to your preferred future

Jonah burns up an incredible amount of emotional energy trying to bring about what he perceives to be a preferred future. He is adamant that things simply must turn out the way he desires, otherwise he will be miserable. Sound familiar?

Many cultures of this world, such as the Philippines, are oriented in the present. Cultures like Britain are past-oriented. Americans are so future-oriented that perhaps our favorite hobby is predicting what will happen next. We are putting our happiness on the gambling table, betting on the slim possibility that the future will unroll itself just exactly as we hope.

Whether it's eager yearning for the future or fretting over its coming, in God's sight it's all as silly as Jonah's temper tantrum. What a waste of emotional energy that could be invested positively. Throw away your crystal ball and trust the future into God's hands. He is totally trustworthy. Hold on loosely to your idea of a perfect future, and just live in expectation of God's next surprise.

What to do with self-pity	What the results will be
See God at work in your circumstances	The joy of the Lord
Let trials build character in you	Fellowship with Christ in His sufferings
Be done with self-absorbed living	God's perspective
Hold on loosely to your picture of a perfect future	Anticipation of God's next surprise

Look at the four results in the right column above. Which one is most lacking in your life?

Now look to the left of that result to see what to do in place of pouting. To overcome self-pity, what specific new habits do you intend to begin today?

Parties are fun, but you surely wouldn't want to have an unending one at your house. One key to having a successful pity party is setting a time limit. Sometimes at the end of a party when guests have lingered long, I want to say as I escort them to the door, "Thank you for *finally* leaving!"

Though a pity party every now and then is a normal human experience, self-pity can become malignant if it lingers long. By the grace of God, determine to end your pity parties quickly. Set a time limit and say, "Self pity, you are no longer a welcomed guest. Thank you for finally leaving. Goodbye!"

When Serving God Brings Out the Very Worst in Me

It was 1990. Auto insurance wasn't yet a real concept in Korea. When there was a collision, the police might eventually weave their way through the traffic jam and arrive at the scene. However, they wouldn't interfere with negotiations. When an accident occurred, the two drivers would get out of their vehicles and fight. Sometimes it was only a verbal attack, but often it became physical as well. Whoever lost the fight had to pay for the repair costs of both vehicles. Thank the Lord Koreans have now discovered both insurance and police authority.

As new missionaries in pre-insurance Korea, Cheryl and I were trained in how to survive car accidents. Foreigners were prime targets for accidents. "Aliens," as foreigners were called, had lots of money and were too polite to win a fight. In our missionary training, we were told to be sure to win the fight.

I soon had an opportunity to prove myself one Sunday after church. Bam! Our new van was suddenly hit by another car. Cheryl was next to me, and the boys were in the back seat. Having seen Koreans in accidents before, I knew the routine.

Out of the van I went. I walked toward the driver's door of the vehicle behind me. Wanting to be sure the driver was startled into surrender, I prepared for a quick attack. As a missionary with culture shock and in language learning stress, I had plenty of pent-up anger needing to be released. Just as I was preparing to open the man's car door and grab him by the neck, I took a look at his face. What a shock! "*Moksanim*!" I was looking into the face of the pastor of the church we had just attended!

Am I all alone in feeling that sometimes serving God brings out the very worst in me? Many missionary friends have assured me that I am not alone. Missionary friends often talk about how serving God in such trying circumstances often brings their personal shortcomings to the surface.

Missionaries try to love people who are very different. They are always giving to others, even when they feel lonely and strung-out. They live among filth, poverty, pollution, noise, and crowds. Language woes will always persist. They are persecuted and misunderstood by the very people they hoped would accept them. Needless to say, missionaries don't wear halos.

It's not just missionaries. Those who have just begun walking with the Lord are often confused by the gap between what was promised to them and what they are now experiencing. They were told to trust in the Lord and He'd provide everything. So they give it a try. What do they find?

They find they have inner battles they never faced before. Temptations increase instead of decrease. Well-meaning Christian friends are now pressuring them to go to more meetings than they have time for, as well as follow a moral code they don't completely understand. They long to live a good life but lack the ability to conquer some sins. Sometimes, the conclusion of the new believer is that serving God brings out the worst in them.

At a minister's luncheon, I asked Ft. Worth, Texas, pastors if they had ever had such feelings.

"There are always committees that feel they must meet," one pastor said. "Deacons want to have the inside scoop on the latest church problem. VDPs (Very Dependent People) want to monopolize my time. Sometimes I want to scream, 'Just bug off! Leave me alone!'"

Serving God brings out the very worst in Jonah too. Actually, it is not that being obedient to the Lord *causes* new character flaws to be formed within Jonah. Serving God puts an extra load on Jonah, revealing and widening pre-existing cracks in Jonah's spiritual foundation. It is the same with us. Serving God has a way of revealing to us areas where we need God's power to change our inner self.

What kind of character flaws are brought to light as Jonah attempts to obey God?

Serving God brings out the prejudice in me

> Then Jonah went out to the east side of the city and made a shelter to sit under as he waited to see if anything would happen to the city. (Jonah 4:5)

Remember that Jonah had declared that in forty days God would destroy Nineveh. But to Jonah's surprise, the people of the city turned from their evil and surrendered themselves to God. What does Jonah do at such a crucial time? He leaves the city! Thousands have repented and are in great need of guidance. The entire nation is experiencing a spiritual breakthrough.

Before his own eyes, Jonah is watching the center of gravity of God's work shift from his own Jewish people to those who were once far away from God. Jonah can't believe his eyes. Until now these people cared nothing about God. They have been cruel to Jonah's own nation, and Jonah considers his own nation as especially favored by God. Suddenly, in one day, these Ninevites repent, and God showers them with his mercy! The thought of it makes Jonah sick.

At this crucial moment in Nineveh, leadership is needed from someone, a flesh-and-blood representative of God's loving mercy. Jonah is God's man of the hour, but he has neither love nor mercy to give. Instead of caring for these repentant people, Jonah skips town.

He leaves the Ninevites at the time of their greatest need. He believes they are unworthy of God's grace and don't deserve Jonah's time. He wants to see them destroyed! So Jonah becomes a vulture. At a distance he impatiently hovers, waiting for death so that he can satisfy himself. *You cruelly killed my people in acts of brutal terror! You are going to die for what you did to my people!*

Am I guilty of picking and choosing the kinds of people who would "make good Christians," then targeting them as the objects of my attention? Am I prone to ignore those who are not attractive to me? Do I go and put an arm around those considered unlovable, or do I seek escape from the burdens and complications of troubled, hurting people?

> Prejudice is … a pernicious disease, especially when found in believers. It can distort our thinking, blind us to what is good and lovely, make us comfortable in our self-complacency, and even harden us towards the spiritual needs of others so that we have no burden for their souls. May the good Lord save us from that. [37]

When Jonah leaves, he goes to the east of the city. Archeologists have excavated the ancient city of Nineveh. They have discovered that the east side of the city is of higher elevation than any other direction out of the city. Jonah sees that higher elevation and chooses to leave by that direction so that he can see clearly the destruction of the entire city. These Ninevites are not his friends. They are the enemies of his own Jewish people. He wants to be an eyewitness to their destruction. He knows God has already listened to their cries of repentance, but he is hoping that maybe, just maybe, God would still judge them.

Now that Jonah has retreated from the place where God is at work, he has too much time on his hands. Maybe his mind wanders back to the past few days he had just spent walking around the city. Those were the good ol' days of yelling in the streets, "Turn or burn!" Jonah regrets that God now seems to be giving these people of Nineveh the option of turning from their ways. Jonah is still looking for the burning to start.

Like Jonah, do you have an eagerness for the judgment of God to fall on unrighteous people? Do you hate sin so much that you also hate the sinner? Can you not see that your own refusal to extend the mercy of God to others is a grave sin?

Do you pull back from people who are richer, poorer, more educated, less educated, from the North, from the South, Democrat, Republican, black, white, or foreign? Do you think they are not worthy of your time?

When God chooses to put into prominence people you would not have chosen, do you rejoice or do you pout?

In the process of serving God, are you discovering that you are prone to decide who is and who isn't worthy of mercy? Like Jonah, are you sometimes ethnocentric, thinking your own kind of people are the best kind of people?

Serving God brings out the desire for short-term pleasure

> Then Jonah…made a shelter to sit under as he waited to see if anything would happen to the city. (Jonah 4:5)

Jonah had just come from his own pity party. He had thrown a temper tantrum before God because God had severely disappointed and embarrassed him.

Waiting for Jonah to calm down, God finally gets a chance to patiently ask Jonah if he was sure he had the right to be angry. Instead of answering God's question, what does Jonah do? He stomps away from God, continuing to pout. Since it is obvious to Jonah that God is going to take care of other people and not Jonah, off he goes to take care of himself.

He builds a simple structure from tree limbs, preparing to wait out the remainder of the thirty-seven days before God will hopefully zap Nineveh with fire from Heaven. In his new shelter, Jonah is all set up for a five-week pity party, which he hopes will be climaxed by the fireworks of Nineveh's total destruction!

Jonah settles into his comfortable nest, perhaps removing a portable hammock from his pocket and extending it between two poles in his shelter.

"This is almost like home. Serving You is not so bad after all, God," Jonah thinks. "The sun is getting hot though. My simple shelter doesn't completely block those rays from my bald head, which got bleached by the enzymes from that fish's belly You stuck me in!"

> Then the Lord God provided a vine and made it grow up over Jonah to give shade for his head to ease his discomfort, and Jonah was very happy about the vine. (Jonah 4:6 NIV)

The vine grew up overnight, offering complete shelter from the sun. For the first time in the Jonah drama, he is happy! You can learn much about people by what makes them happy and sad.

"God, you've finally done something for *me*! I still can't forgive You for being gracious to those people, but at least I can thank you for being gracious to *me*," Jonah prays. "To be honest God, I don't enjoy serving You, and I sure don't care about other people, but I enjoy the fringe benefits You provide."

Answer these questions:
- Do you find more pleasure in the gifts God gives you than in God Himself?
- Are you content in your own comfort while an entire city around you is in need of care?
- Does your desire for short-term personal pleasure rob you of being who God wants you to be?
- By your lifestyle, which of these two things are you putting as priority: creature comfort or sacrificial service? The provision or the Provider? Comfort or God's plan?

If God sees that you delight more in the shade of a vine than in Him, He may take away your vine!

> But God also prepared a worm! The next morning at dawn the worm ate through the stem of the plant, so that it soon died and withered away. And as the sun grew hot, God sent a scorching east wind to blow on Jonah. The sun beat down on his head until he grew faint and wished to die. (Jonah 4:7–8)

The vine sprang up in one day, and in even less time a worm nibbled at the vine's stem, completely severing and killing the vine. God knew exactly how much it would take to get Jonah's attention. A worm eating his vine is barely enough to wake up Jonah from his pleasant siesta.

God not only causes Jonah's treasured vine to die, He causes a scorching east wind to blow Jonah's blessings away! Now, the heat is wilting Jonah. Desert sand dust is blowing into his eyes. Jonah is about to faint. Forget all about Jonah being happy. Now Jonah is mad again.

When God chooses not to favor you while He favors others, what is your response? One response would be to turn away from Him. Another response is to realize He may just be trying to get your attention long enough to teach you something about yourself. Do you really expect that following God will make you safe and secure from all alarms? God never promised us an easy life. *God is not into your comfort nearly so much as He is into your obedience.*

Serving the Lord in today's world can be really tough. Demands are placed on your time. You are constantly stretched almost beyond your level of elasticity. You seldom "leave the job." You would just once like to finish a task, look at the final product, wash your hands of it, and go home feeling like you can completely relax. Serving God is a 24/7 job. It doesn't provide immediate results. Sometimes serving God leaves you frustrated and wanting to look for short-term pleasure fixes.

Jonah had the pleasure of a vine for one day. Are you seeking one-day pleasures in inappropriate ways? Do you look for pleasurable but inappropriate viewing on the Internet? Do you have more passion for your own comfort than you have for other people?

When Jonah loses his vine, he has a meltdown. What is your vine? What is for you the thing that, if God were to take it away, your world would crumble apart?

Jonah sees the loss of his personal shade tree as a terrible catastrophe, while the loss of a whole city to the wrath of God is a cause for celebration. Jonah cares more about the vine than he does for an entire nation.

Whenever serving God brings out my desire for short-term pleasure, I lose my perspective on what brings true, lasting satisfaction.

Serving God brings out the self-absorption in me

> It is better for me to die than to live. (Jonah 4:8 KJV)

"It is better for me."

Does Jonah *really* know what is better for him? Self-absorption is a lifestyle that bases all decisions on what is better for me, not on what is good for others. Where does such a lifestyle lead? Most of the time it doesn't deliver the better life I expected.

Where does self-absorption take Jonah? The "it is better for me" approach to life repeatedly makes Jonah want, or *think* he wants, to die. Because he felt it was better to die than obey God, he told the sailors to throw him overboard. How fortunate that God does not permit what Jonah thinks is best. Because he is mad at God for being kind to the Ninevites, Jonah tells God to kill him, but still God does not give Jonah his request.

"It is better for me to die." In this Hebrew phrase, Jonah is actually commanding himself to quit breathing. The literal Hebrew wording says, "Self, die!" Talk about a death wish! Does Jonah really know what is best for self? Do you?

Self-absorbed living has me more concerned with me than the spiritual condition of those around me. When I am consumed with what is better for me, my happiness depends on my circumstances. I am happy with the shelter and the vine. Bring a worm and strong winds my way, and I want to show God and everyone else just how close to death I really am.

When serving God brings out the self-absorption in you, you will think that life is meaningless. This happens because you realize life really isn't about you. You may even slip into suicidal depression. When the "it is better for me" mindset has taken over, you rob yourself of experiencing God's best for you. The inner turmoil of conflicting values starts to kill you inside.

What happens if God leaves you alone to do whatever you think is better for you? You may create a temporary haven of shelter for yourself, enjoy its shade for a while, and even deceive yourself into thinking it is all Heaven-sent.

> When life is tranquil, relationships intact, finances secure, and physical health flourishing; when the enemy is not at the gate; when the war drums are not rattling; when the Calvin Klein perfume advertisement for Eternity for Men seems plausible—then a sense of complacency, self-sufficiency, and personal command of one's destiny deludes and lulls us.[38]

Fortunately, God is not content to leave you alone to do whatever seems better to you. He creates uncomfortable situations that bring into clear light the conflict of values you were hoping to keep hidden deep in your heart. When serving God brings out the self-absorption in you, God gets the opportunity to shake up your life.

What are you learning about yourself so far?

There is only one letter difference between self and elf. The Jonah approach to life makes you really small. It reduces you to misery and causes you to wilt away in the sun even while those around you are enjoying revival with God. When you attempt to serve God but end up in self-absorption, it becomes almost impossible to trust God for what is truly best.

Serving God brings out the stubbornness in me

> Then God said to Jonah, "Is it right for you to be angry because the plant died?"
> "Yes," Jonah retorted, "even angry enough to die!" (Jonah 4:9)

God is patiently trying to teach Jonah an extremely important lesson, but to the very end, Jonah stubbornly refuses to change his mind. At the end of the story, Jonah is even more stubborn than when he started.

Self-importance does not allow any challenge to my integrity. If someone asks me about a weakness, I become defensive. "How dare you question my motives! I have a good heart. I am who I am, so just accept me for me," I might say.

When serving God brings out the stubbornness in you, there is no room for change. Your thoughts are distorted, so things look different than they actually are. You feel that *you* don't need to change, but of course other people surely do. They have lots of room for improvement, and some of them have a really long way to go. And God? Surely He sees how much farther ahead you are compared with those lesser than you, right? If you remain determined to win Him over to your way, maybe one day God will see things as clearly as you do.

God continues in patient appeal for stubborn Jonah to change.

> Then the Lord said, "You feel sorry about the plant, though you did nothing to put it there. And a plant is only, at best, short lived. But Nineveh has more than 120,000 people living in spiritual darkness, not to mention all the animals. Shouldn't I feel sorry for such a great city? (Jonah 4:10–11)

Jonah is passionate about *his* shelter he made for himself, the comfort *he* experiences, and the nice vine God provides for *him*. In contrast, God is passionate about the spiritual condition of all people.

God is trying to move Jonah's passion along from plants to animals and then on to people. "Jonah, you love a one-day personal comfort more than the Kingdom. Look at all these people, Jonah. Please, love them with me," God pleads.

Jonah stubbornly refuses. He does not want his heart to beat as one with the heart of God. His only passion is self. To the very end, Jonah is stubborn and unchanging before God. You may think you are not like Jonah, but Jonah didn't see himself as self-absorbed either.

When serving God brings out the stubbornness in you, you are rebelling against God's attempts to change who you are.

In what areas of your life are you stubborn? How has your stubbornness shown itself lately?

Whenever you become serious about serving God, your own character flaws may become more evident. When serving God just seems to bring out the very worst in you, what should you do? Should you just drop the thought of following Him and live for self, just like everyone else in this world? Before you give up so easily, take a look at the self-centered people around you. Do you really want to become like them and like Jonah? Let God work on your character, and stop living for self. The more you focus on self, the more the problem is perpetuated. Go out and start helping people in need.

When you don't like what the demands of service to God are revealing about the condition of your inner man, instead of giving up or giving in, you should pray.

Pray this prayer right now:

God, when serving You brings out the prejudice in me, help me to see all people through Your eyes of compassionate mercy. God, help me to love people who, until now, I have considered unworthy of my time and affection.

When serving You brings out from within me a desire for short-term pleasure, may I find true, lasting delight in who You are. Take my passion for things that cannot satisfy, and re-create me into someone who takes great pleasure in serving You. Let my desire for quick satisfaction be a reminder that I need to feast more often on the more satisfying nourishment found in You.

When serving You brings out the self-absorption in me, I pray that I will clearly see the misery and death that living in Me-ville brings. Make me selfless. I want to die to self so that I can live for You. You must increase. I must decrease, to the point that I no longer control my life, but You live in and through me, controlling every thought.

When serving you brings out the stubbornness in me, I pray that You would strip me of all that is still left of self will, so that I stand transparent before You. Reveal to me any stubbornly unclean places in my heart, soul, mind, and body. Renew a right spirit within me so that I can be useful in reaching my Nineveh for Your Kingdom.

Amen.

Developing a Heart for My City

JONAH IS RELUCTANT TO GO the city, but he finally goes, fully determined to get out of Nineveh as quickly as he can. It's easy to understand why Jonah has an allergy to the city. I've been to some interesting cities in the world. However, most of the cities are crowded, polluted, and frustrating. The city is often the last place I'd want be!

How would you like to live in Beijing, China? You're probably thinking about the Great Wall, Tiananmen Square, and the Forbidden City. Those are key aspects of the city, but what you probably aren't aware of is the hours you'll spend in traffic getting to these tourist attractions.

In a Chinese city, the car horn is an absolute essential tool for survival. Correct use of the horn means honking as often as possible to let everyone know you are coming!

As the Chinese learn to drive, as only some truly do, frequent use of the horn is drilled in to their psyche. Here is one of the many horn-related questions on the Beijing driving exam:

355. When driving through a residential area, you should

a) honk like normal.
b) honk more than normal, in order to alert residents.
c) avoid honking, in order to avoid disturbing the residents.[39]

The correct answer is: b) honk more than normal!

Despite our inclinations to avoid noisy cities, cities are on God's heart. The particular city where you live is on God's heart; is it on yours? When God looks at the city, He feels deep compassion for the multitudes of people living there.

> Shouldn't I feel sorry for such a great city? (Jonah 4:11)

God is deeply concerned about the great cities of the world; cities teeming with people in need of Him. However, we tend to be like Jonah. We have either chosen not to share God's word in our city, or we give mere lip service for God as we pass through the city as quickly as we can. If God is concerned with the cities, why aren't we?

Imagine how exciting it would be to serve as the U.S. ambassador for a world-class city like Singapore—a place where people from all over the world come to work and live. The classy, clean city is alive with the aroma of foods and with people from all corners of the globe.

Our missionary kid niece Tessa loved living in Beijing. Yes, living in a city of millions had its frustrations, but there was something that made her feel she was a part of something bigger. To survive in a city, Tessa needed to find her niche, an area where she belonged and could make a difference. In a city, you can either get lost, or you can find out who you really are.

Cities are living, breathing organisms, a microcosm of nations and humanity. Living in the city can be exciting, invigorating, and challenging.

Just like Nineveh, cities like Singapore, Hong Kong, New York, Tokyo, Los Angeles, and Vancouver have huge Kingdom potential, because what happens there affects the entire world. This is why cities are on God's heart. Cities dictate economic growth, politics, fashion, and commerce. They also play a huge role for the spread of values and religious beliefs to surrounding cities and countries.

Like Jonah, you have a divine appointment as God's ambassador to reach your city. How thrilling to be chosen as an ambassador of the Kings of kings in your modern-day Nineveh!

What do you need to do to prepare? Well, first you must pray. Let's start with this prayer:

In this era of rapid urbanization, God, give me your heart for the city! May my heart beat as one with Your heart of compassion for the multitudes of people in this city.

When Jonah finds out he is Nineveh's ambassador, he does not pray. He is selected to be the ambassador for the key city of the world's most powerful region. God is counting on Jonah to represent Him in a matter where thousands of lives are at stake. Yet Jonah has no heart for the city.

He has a heart for his own village and his own people. Jonah was from a little laid-back village with an obscure name: Gath-hepher. Only those few Bubbas who are from Gath-hepher have ever heard of it! We each tend to get one location locked into our hearts. God comes along and tries to put a more Kingdom-strategic place on our hearts, but we choose instead to stay in our own little Gath-hepher.

> Nineveh has more than 120,000 people living in spiritual darkness … Shouldn't I feel sorry for such a great city? (Jonah 4:11)

Do you have a heart for the city? Why or why not?

What keeps Jonah from having a heart for Nineveh? What was the city of Nineveh like? Nineveh was such a grand place that perhaps the complexity of such a busy, bustling city was a threat to country-boy Jonah. He probably feared that he'd lose himself in the city.

Do we fear the complexity of the city?

Nineveh was located on the east bank of the Tigris River, which is across from modern day Mosul, Iraq. Several times in the Jonah drama, God describes Nineveh using the word "great."

> Get up and go to the great city… (Jonah 1:2)
> Get up and go to the great city… (Jonah 3:2–3)

Whenever God repeats Himself, it's because He wants to make clear to us what's on His heart. Whenever He speaks to Jonah, it's always something about Jonah's responsibility for this great city. God makes it clear that He has a heart for the great city of Nineveh. He still has a heart for cities just like it today. God speaks to us today about our responsibility for the cities of the world. Will we hear His voice?

Nineveh was, for many reasons, truly a great city, as modern excavation has demonstrated. Some of what was unearthed has been placed in the British Museum in London. The excavation revealed some fascinating facts about the great city of Nineveh.

An ancient hunter whose name was Nimrod founded Nineveh.[40] Since its founding, Nineveh maintained a reputation of being very brutal. The Assyrians of Nineveh stuck their victims on sharp poles and left them to roast to death in the desert sun. They also beheaded people by the thousands and stacked their skulls up in piles at the city gates.[41] Sometimes, they buried people in the desert, leaving only their heads above ground. They would stretch out the enemies' tongues, run a stake through them, and then leave them to die. We can see why Jonah was a bit reluctant to go to a place like Nineveh.

The main gate of the city put fear into anyone considering entrance. Not only did stacks of enemy skulls guard the gate, statues of winged bulls lined each side. Winged bulls were also found guarding other parts of the city. These bulls were some of the many gods worshipped by the people of Nineveh.

Archeologists found the remains of a wall fifty feet across and more than one hundred feet high encircling the city. Built by Nineveh ruler Sennacherib, these walls extended far underground to also prohibit the possibility of enemies digging under.

It was also discovered that although the city within the walls was very sizeable, the outlying area beyond the walls was even greater. In this outer part of the city, archeologists discovered fruit orchards, water conduits for irrigation, exotic plantations, and more than a thousand corn fields.

In 1850, the library of Nineveh was excavated. This building was guarded on either side by figures of "Ea," the god of culture. The library contained tablets of clay covering topics such as grammar, astronomy, music, law, science, history, commerce, and liturgies, rituals and hymns for worshipping various gods.[42]

Though the book of Jonah does not say much about Nineveh's wickedness, there were other prophets who lived around the same time as Jonah—prophets like Joel, Amos, and Nahum. They describe Nineveh as guilty of evil plots against God, taking advantage of the helpless, cruelty in war, idolatry, prostitution, and witchcraft.[43]

The complexity of such a city may have been just too much for Jonah, son of Amittai, from little Gath-hepher. In the village of Gath-hepher, giving a bath to a heifer may have been the highlight of the day, so going to a city with decapitated heads as trophies and learned scholars discussing the latest ideas wasn't something Jonah could fathom doing. He felt out of his league. He knew he'd be lost in translation—or headless.

Today's cities are certainly just as complex as Nineveh was. Cheryl and I have spent twenty years of our lives living in high-rise apartment complexes in cities in East Asia. In these cities, we have seen people squatting on the street to urinate and defecate. We have inhaled pollution so thick that visibility is reduced to a few feet, causing police to halt all traffic until the wind begins to blow.

We have also felt some of the fear Jonah must have felt going into an enemy city. While living in an East Asian city, our relationship with Christ was thought of by authorities as spiritual pollution. We were occasionally followed by government information gatherers. One day at a wedding, a group of policemen sought information from me by trying to get me drunk. They actually pried open my jaw and were about to force the liquid down my throat! How thankful I was for our son Jonathan coming to my rescue. Standing six feet three inches tall, he boldly towered himself above the little Asian policemen, who quickly whimpered away.

It seems that in the city, everyone is wishing they were someplace else. They walk fast to get to that other place and talk on the cell phone with people in that other place. Technology helps people feel connected in a highly impersonal environment, even if their connection is only digital.

In the city, you can be whoever you want to be. You can change your look and pretend to be any number of personas. People move to cities to find themselves, yet many people wind up losing themselves. What is the remedy to this? You have to know who you are when you move to the city. Otherwise trying to find yourself in the city is like searching for Waldo.

I took my son Joshua with me on a ministry trip to a factory in a large industrial city of East Asia. We slept in the factory dorm, where they sleep eight workers to the room. Beds, which are stacked on top of each other in sets of four, consist of sheets of plywood without mattresses. There are open-air windows with no screens, so mosquitoes have free rein at night. The only good news is that that the pollution is so bad it kills most of the mosquitoes.

When Joshua and I woke up in the dorm, the first thing we saw in the room was a rat. The Bible says we should give thanks in all things, so we gave thanks that the rat was a dead rat! Getting serious about reaching our cities involves sacrifice, but may result in the joy of a great harvest.

In East Asia, rural families lack even survival-level income. Young people leave their families behind in remote villages, and with teary eyes, they depart for the distant city to look for any available work. They will send their entire salary back to their hungry village family. Factories hire them for less than two hundred American dollars per month, and then require them to pay for their own space in a crowded dorm room. Workers also buy their own food in the factory mess hall, where sanitation or nutrition is not much of a concern.

Lonely, hungry, and searching for answers, when rural migrants come to the city factories, some of them hear about Jesus for the first time. They are looking for an identity.

Ah Feng grew up in the harshest of circumstances, never having enough food. At the age of nineteen, she migrated to a factory, where she experienced the love of Christian fellowship. There she found Christ and has been sharing Him with others ever since. Thousands of new churches are springing up within the city factories of East Asia. God is at work in the city!

Will you join God as He targets the city with His love and mercy? Or will the complexity of the city overwhelm you?

Do I have more compassion for my own home than I do for the people in my city?

Jonah wants to watch the commotion of the city, but he wants to do so from a suburban distance. He builds his home away from all the noise of the city and is thrilled that God has blessed him with a vine to surround his castle and add to his comfort. Jonah decides city life isn't so bad, as long as he can live in the privacy of his own little suburban palace.

However, when a worm suddenly devours the once beautiful landscape of Jonah's private yard, the value of Jonah's home drastically decreases. This turn of events reveals where Jonah's passion is: his own home. God has orchestrated it all to contrast Jonah's compassion for his own castle to God's compassion for the city.

> You feel sorry about the plant ... Shouldn't I feel sorry for such a great city? (Jonah 4:10–11)

It took God longer to get Jonah to go to the great city than it took the entire godless city of Nineveh to repent. While we criticize Jonah for his unwillingness to get involved in Nineveh, we must ask ourselves why we are so reluctant to reach the cities of our world today.

Though we describe the cities as spiritually unresponsive, as oppressive, and as evil strongholds, our perception may show more about our fear of the city than it does the city's readiness to respond to the Lord. Many Christians living in so-called unresponsive cities find that when they care about the people there, they discover an openness to God's love among city dwellers. One thing the story of Jonah makes clear to us: *cities are neglected places where a great number of people can be reached for the Kingdom if we will simply go and share God's word with hearts of compassion.*

One reason we are reluctant to reach our cities is because we would rather escape from them into our own castles. Our homes are safer, nicer, and more comfortable. The city is sometimes not so comfortable. So, we drive thirty minutes or more out of the city to the quiet suburb, where we punch the garage door opener, pull into our castle, close the door behind us, and pamper ourselves with the fast food we bought in a drive-through window. The quiet seclusion of our private cave and the fences that protect us from others cause us to forget we have responsibility to serve God by reaching out to our urban and suburban neighbors.

What if God were to radically change your life, uproot you from the comforts of your home, and relocate you to a city where you must relate to people who are drastically different from you? How would you respond?

It's not just you and me who want to escape the city. Churches have done the same.

Many churches that were originally built in growing cities now find themselves in transitional communities, which often cause them to want to run from the city. Instead, God calls churches to embrace the inner city.

It is possible to maintain a vibrant inner-city church campus and ministry while at the same time creating a new suburban campus and ministry. However, many churches elect to run to the suburbs and abandon their former inner city locations. Do we love the inner-city people of our Nineveh, or do we flee from the city?

Does my church reach only those in the city who are *my* kind of people? Have we somehow convinced ourselves we are not responsible for people who are not like us? If "they" become larger in number than "us," will we relocate our church from the city to the suburb where our kind of people now live?

Love has no color, income, fashion, or culture. Love transcends these divisions. Love has no division. If we are going to call ourselves the body of Christ, why don't we love like God loves? Perhaps one of the largest barriers between Christians and non-Christians is Christian hypocrisy. We don't practice what we preach. We are not inclusive. We do not love unconditionally. We are not humble.

I now pastor in the city of Albany, Georgia, where the population is split 60 percent black and 40 percent white. Seldom do the two mix. Most whites live in plush, suburban Northwest Albany, while most blacks live in the poverty-stricken southeast part of the city.

Recently, a group of young Christian men dared to claim part of Albany city for the Kingdom. They opened up a dorm in an area known for violence and crime. These men now live in the dorm and provide lifestyle mentoring to troubled young men, many of whom eagerly accept guidance from those willing to live among them.

To reach the peoples whom the American church has been avoiding, the church needs to exist among those peoples. No one wants an outsider coming in and acting like they have all the answers. Living in the same environment brings credibility and allows relationships to form.

Do I have more compassion for my own pets than I do for the people of my city?

Pets are great. As humans, we can really become attached to our pets. We tend to be more loyal to them than to other people. This is probably because they don't wound us like humans often do. Pets are blindly loyal.

God first makes an appeal to Jonah about the huge loss of life that would happen in Nineveh. That doesn't work, so God uses a plant to appeal to Jonah. When that doesn't work either, God appeals to Jonah through a concern for animals. God is trying to move Jonah's passion from plants to animals and then along to *people*.

> Nineveh has more than 120,000 people ... not to mention all the animals. (Jonah 4:11)

God may be thinking, "Well, if Jonah's heart is unmoved by statistics about numbers of lost people, I will show him the pitiful condition of the animals there. Maybe that will move him to have a heart for the city."

Pets are awesome! Let's see, there was Shep, a German shepherd I loved in elementary school. Then there was Kung Fu, the Siamese cat who entertained me as an adolescent. Then there was Dapper Doo, the mutt who was my companion during lonely days before marriage. These and other animals were close to my heart.

Most of us have cried over a lost pet. Perhaps we can even remember a funeral we conducted for a favorite pet. We love our animals. If we see abused or neglected animals, we feel very sad. We create organizations to protect animal rights. If our dog gets run over by a car, we don't just sit back and say, "Well, doggone!" When we lose a pet, our natural, human response is to weep. How long has it been since we wept over the lost condition of our city?

A television script for a nature program that I saw recently said that animals are equal with people. Is that right thinking? While we should care for animals, do we really care as much about animals as we do people?

Dying animals often go off by themselves. However, people who are spiritually dying often flock to the cities. What has happened to our concern for the hurting multitudes coming into our cities?

What are the names of some of your favorite pets?

Do you have more compassion for these animals than you do for the people of your city? What are the names of five people in spiritual darkness in your city?

Will I begin to see the world through God's urban-focused eyes?

> ... 120,000 people living in spiritual darkness ... such a great city ... (Jonah 4:11)

When God looks at the city, what does He see? Of course He sees dead rats, trash, noise, and drugs. These conditions are of concern to Him. However, what is it that God sees that really tugs at His heart? It is city *people*: urban dwellers living in spiritual darkness.

When God looks at the city, He doesn't have to count the number of people there. Notice that God already knows the exact population of Nineveh. Numbers are important to Him because numbers represent people. When we are determining where we should share the Gospel, we must place priority on places where there are the greatest numbers of people. As simple as that sounds, we have somehow gotten sidetracked away from doing missions in the cities.

A few decades ago, mission strategists studied the unreached people groups (UPGs) of the world. They pinpointed on a large world map the locations of hundreds of ethnic groups untouched by the message of Christ. As a result, mission organizations sent record numbers of missionaries out to try to find these very remote people groups.

While there was some validity to this emphasis, what actually happened was that missionaries were sent out to target UPGs of say, ten thousand people, while cities of a million or more people had no Gospel witness at all.

Still today, in China there are more than a hundred cities, each with a population of one million or more, where fewer than 1 percent of the population are believers, and yet there is virtually no Gospel witness.[44] Perhaps through your influence, God will lead your church to adopt one of these cities. Perhaps one of them is your Nineveh.[45]

It's time now for our mission strategy to catch up with God's heart. Where will we find Him today? In this world of rapid urbanization, we find Him following His heart to the city. He has a heart of compassion for the great urban centers where the people are.

When God looks at the city, He checks the spiritual condition of the people there and sees the multitudes living in spiritual darkness. Do you see with God's eyes the spiritual condition of your city? Will you lead people in your church to prayer-walk and prayer-drive through your city, praying for God to show you the spiritual condition of the people there? Maybe you should make a spiritual map of your city, showing places of poverty, affluence, immorality, disease, extravagance, and desperation. Surely God will lead you to do something about the spiritual condition of your city.

Though you may not live in a famous, world-class city, God sees the city where you live as having strategic Kingdom value. There are multitudes of hurting people in your city who need you to be God's ambassador to them. Your city is on God's heart.

What will I do to reach my city?

As a teenager in Jackson, Mississippi, Brantley went on a mission trip to Nairobi. For the first time in his life, he saw muddy streets, hovering flies, and dreary huts made out of dried cow dung. He noticed there were often six or more people and many animals living together in one small hut. The experience opened his eyes to the needs of others.

After returning home to Mississippi, he began to see his own city with new eyes. There were many similarities between the African huts and the ramshackle houses of Jackson's ghettos. He had never noticed them before. Brantley did some research and found that he was living near some of the worst poverty and urban rot in the United States. His heart was moved to do something about it.

"Jesus often treated physical needs before He attended spiritual needs," Brantley says. "It's hard for a person to get serious about heaven if he's starving."[46] So Brantley, as a teenager, launched a nonprofit charity to help needy families in Mississippi. Students Aiding Indigent Families (SAIF) purchases abandoned houses in Jackson's slums, recruits teams of students to repair and remodel them into like-new condition, and offers financing to the new owner. Poor, single mothers purchase most of the homes. Brantley describes fun as serving others, making a difference, and pleasing God.

What will you do to reach your city? There is great power in the unity of God's people working together across denominational and ethnic lines to reach the entire city for the Lord. We must work together with other believers to transform our cities for Christ.

What can you do? Start by turning your private castle into a place with an open door of care for your neighbors. Partner with other believers to care about the people of your city. Together, meet practical needs to show God's love. There are people in your city who need you to teach them English. You can also fix furniture, help people move in or out of homes, invite people to your home to eat, host fun celebrations and informative seminars, as well as celebrate seasons and holidays as opportunities to show tangible care for the people of your city.[47]

In some cities, such as Dallas, Texas, believers of all denominations and ethnicity are gathering together to pray for spiritual revival of their urban area. On May 5, 2009, under the banner "God of this City," more than thirty thousand diverse Christians gathered in a Dallas stadium for the sole purpose of praying for God to use them to transform their city. Now many of them are living out their prayers by becoming the hands and feet of Jesus in the city.

Jonah is not a good example of having a heart for the city. Fortunately, One greater than Jonah is here. Jonah looks over the city of Nineveh and grieves that a repentant city is spared. In Luke 13:34-35, Jesus looks over the city of Jerusalem and grieves that an unrepentant city must be judged.

What about you? Will you look at the city through the eyes of Jesus or the eyes of Jonah? May the limits of your compassion be determined by Jesus, not by Jonah!

Where Is God When I Am Self-Absorbed?

IN THE BOOK *A FAREWELL to Arms*, Ernest Hemingway explores his own view of the nature of God, whom he likens to an indifferent bystander. The main character in the book is Fred Henry, who spends his days fishing and his nights sitting by the campfire drinking whiskey.

One night, when Fred puts another log on the campfire, thousands and thousands of ants come streaming out of the log, scurrying from one end of the burning log to the other. He thinks to himself, *I could take the log off the fire and save those ants, but I don't want to.* Hemingway uses this illustration to suggest that God is indifferent toward hurting people.

Where is God when I am self-absorbed? When I am running from one end of life to the other like I'm on fire, does God even care? I might think, like Hemingway did, that God is letting me burn.

When I am self-absorbed, I would rather pick on God. It's fun to accuse Him of not caring about me, but the truth is that when I am self-absorbed, God is vigorously pursuing me, drawing me and others back to Him.[48]

The Jonah in each of us is too dazed and crazed to even see God right before our eyes. We are so busy running around to see that God is patiently waiting on us to have a heart-to-heart talk with Him.

Are there aspects of your life about which you would rather not have an open conversation with God? Do you limit God's influence over your life by keeping from Him your fantasies, fears, and joys? Why do you not let Him in on what's going on in your heart? Is it because you believe God is too busy with more important things to respond to your emotional state?

It takes great effort for God to free you from self-absorption. The absolutely amazing thing is that when you are self-absorbed, God still *wants* to relate to you! The real question is not, "Where is God?" but, "While God is chasing after you, where are you?"

God is mentioned thirty-eight times in Jonah, while the name "Jonah" is mentioned less than half that number. This is less a story about Jonah and more a story about God responding to self-absorbed Jonah. Take God out of the story and it doesn't make sense. In each scene of Jonah's story, God is doing something great, helping free Jonah and others from self-absorption.

Just to lay aside all doubt about where God is when you are living for you, let's take one final overview of the Jonah story. Let's see if God is, as so many who don't even know Him suppose, indifferently drunk beside His big campfire somewhere out there in the sky.

Where is God when I am self-absorbed?

He is calling me to live beyond my self

> The Lord gave this message to Jonah ..." Get up and go to ... Nineveh!" ... But Jonah got up and went in the opposite direction ... (Jonah 1:1,3)

At the very time we might expect a human father to baby us, protect us, and assure us he would never make a difficult demand on us, what does our Heavenly Father do? He pushes the baby bird out of the bird's nest and says, "Get up and go!"

Have you had this happen to you?

When I am idle, minding my own business—just like any normal, self-absorbed person would do, out of the blue, God challenges me to fulfill a humongous task. He sends me a job description that makes me wonder if He got confused about who to send it to. It's obviously way beyond what I am capable of. What is He thinking?

Doesn't He know that, just like Jonah, I have already been so many places for Him and obeyed Him so many times before?[49] This time He's just asking too much. I deserve a break today from serving Him. I have already sacrificed a lot. Like Jonah, I feel I have earned a vacation cruise.

Jonah may very well have said to the Lord, "Doesn't my record of previous usefulness to You make my current unwillingness acceptable? Isn't there an exemption clause somewhere in my contract? My Father's name is 'Amitai,' meaning faithful or true, so why don't you send someone like him? He's a better man than me. Why me? Why now? Why Nineveh?"

God certainly would have been justified in choosing someone else instead of Jonah. Most humans would have given up on Jonah a long time ago, but God does not.

Why does God choose me instead of someone else? Because the tough task God puts on self-absorbed me will force me into a life of dependence on Him. The task will also force me to get my focus off self, so I should not cringe when God calls me to do something very difficult.

Imagine God saying to you, "Go to the enemy country. Tell them I am the one true God. Tell them to turn to me before it's too late. Now get up, and go tell them." How would you react?

How do you respond to God's call to do difficult things for him? Do you cringe at His voice? Do you avoid His glance, and run to Tarshish if He calls you to Nineveh? Do you dismiss the possibility of simply trusting in His goodness by simply going where He says go? Do you see His mercy and grace as theological truths but not something you must offer to all peoples of the earth?

When you are self-absorbed, it seems crazy, but God wants to send you to the most spiritually dark corner of your neighborhood or perhaps the Earth. Going where there is no knowledge of who the Lord is will show you the bigger picture: life isn't all about you. There's nothing like mission service to overcome self-absorption in a hurry. Go to the mission field and experience first-hand the joy of being a small light, shining brightly in vast darkness.

In our Western world, we choose who we will love, then try to love our choice. In societies like Korea, many marriages are arranged, especially among the middle and upper class. I remember during Korean language school, my Korean tennis partner invited me to his wedding.

He had never mentioned her before, so I asked him, "How long have you known her?"

He replied, "I only saw her across the room one time last month, but our families have decided we are right for each other." Though having love chosen for us seems strange, low divorce rates show the merit of arranged marriages.

Even today in many Eastern societies, the one you will love is chosen for you, and then you learn to love the one chosen for you. For the Christian, God chooses who we are to love. We are to love those He loves. God so loved *the world* ..." Though the Jonah in us wants to pick and choose who we will and will not love, God has chosen for us to love all people of the world. Will we obey and learn to love His choice for us?

God is at work to cure you of self-absorption and is calling you to be on mission with Him. Trust Him and accept the new job description to love all people as He does.

Where is God when I am self-absorbed?

He is challenging me to get honest about who I am

> The Lord flung a powerful wind over the sea ... All this time, Jonah was sound asleep down in the hold ...
> "How can you sleep at a time like this? ... Get up and pray ..."
> (Jonah 1:4–6)

Do I know who I really am?

When I am restless and running from my own shadow, God brings me to a point of forced, honest appraisal of who I have become. I must honestly admit that though He has never once turned His back on me, I have repeatedly turned my back on God.

Jonah is a stowaway with an unknown past. The sailors on the ship have no idea who Jonah really is, because Jonah has deliberately concealed his identity.

We're in the same boat as Jonah. We would rather hide our identity as a godly person than risk being made fun of or maybe even being thrown off the friendship boat. We wouldn't dare risk appearing in public as people who serve our God, so we decide to just be closet Christians, hiding down in the safe hull of our sanctuaries. It's certainly easier and more comfortable that way.

The world will not tolerate such hypocrisy for long. Hypocrisy is being pointed out in the American church. People are coming down to where we are hiding, slapping us in the face, and saying, "Don't you know we're in a crisis here? Get up and pray! Be who you say you are!"

Finally Jonah stops his hypocrisy and reveals his identity. He says, "I worship Elohim," a name so holy that it is seldom spoken. It referred to the all powerful, sovereign Creator of heaven and earth.

Throughout all of this, God is challenging Jonah to be honest about who he is. Notice all the ways God tries to get Jonah's attention. He sends a powerful wind followed by a violent storm, and then sends a great fish, and finally, God creates a vine and a worm to eat it. These are all miraculous acts of God attempting to teach Jonah something about self-absorption.

Sometimes God allows suffering in your life to teach you something about your own need for character development. The root of one of the Hebrew words for suffering means "to educate." Sometimes God educates you in old-school ways.

C.S. Lewis said, "God whispers to us in health and prosperity, but being hard of hearing, we fail to hear God's voice in both ... God turns up the amplifier by means of suffering. Then His voice booms."[50]

When you are self-absorbed, God is at work to get your attention and to challenge you to face up to the facts about yourself. Are you hard of hearing? How loud does God have to turn up the amplifier of suffering before you begin to listen? What is He saying to you now about your character?

Where is God when I am self-absorbed?

He is drawing people to Himself, despite me

> They cried out to the Lord, Jonah's God ... The sailors were awestruck by the Lord's great power, and they ... vowed to serve Him. (Jonah 1:13, 16)

When I am oblivious to any higher purpose for my life, God is drawing people to Himself through me, or more accurately, despite me. Though God is certainly not pleased with my disobedience, He can still use the situation to bring glory to Himself.

Even through Jonah's identity crisis on the ship, God is at work showing His great power to the sailors. They in turn give up their idols and believe in the one true God.

When Jonah finally arrives at Nineveh, he goes through the motions of obedience. Even though Jonah's heart is not in it, God still uses Jonah to cause a whole city to turn to Him. Isn't it amazing what God does through us despite us?

Has there been a time when God did something unexpected through you, even though at the time you were not really on the best of terms with God?

God is able to use even your mistakes and half-hearted obedience to help others come to know Him. He can use you even when you are not willing. It's not about you and your striving for perfection. It's about God working out His purposes through imperfect you. Remember: He doesn't need you, but chooses to use you.

Where is God when I am self-absorbed?

He is delivering me from self-destruction

> I called to you from the world of the dead, and Lord, you heard me! (Jonah 2:2)

When I am as low as I could possibly go and hoping to end it all, God is rescuing me before I hurt myself.

Notice God doesn't ever remind Jonah of his disobedience, or rub Jonah's flightiness in his face. We do that well enough to ourselves. When the errors are as big as Jonah's, humans don't tend to give second chances. But God is beyond human, and He gives Jonah chance after chance without even saying, "Jonah, this is your final chance." God is the God of seventy times seven chances.

Was there a time in your life when you did not deserve a second chance but got one anyway?

God gives Jonah lots of concrete evidence that Jonah, despite his failures, is still deeply loved. Do you really know and understand that God loves you, not just when you succeed, but even when you fail?

Tessa is afraid of failure. She knows she is called to write, but usually not a day goes by that she doesn't worry that she will fail at what she loves to do. The fear of failure is a failure to see God as omnipotent. To fear failure is to see ourselves as in charge and capable of screwing up God's plan. If we are in the center of God's will, we need not fear failing.

Where is God when you feel you are failing? In the belly of your whale of self-absorption, remember the Lord and turn back to Him. The only reason you even ask the question, "Where is God?" is because you are far from Him.

Take heart—God is your deliverer! So many things have held you captive that you have become a slave, chained by your own desires. Suddenly, into your dark dungeon comes your rescuer, breaking your chains and setting you free from self. He empowers you through His Spirit to live not for self, but for God.

Hallelujah! When you are self-absorbed, God is working hard to deliver you from self-destruction. Your Deliverer rescues you from you! You are free to say, "Yes, there is more to life than me."

In Jesus Christ, find the bigger picture. Live in community with people who are authentically sharing life with each other and who are together serving God by reaching the people of Nineveh. Such a life is so drastically different from a life of lonely self-destruction.

Has there been a time in your life when you had self-destructive habits? How was your merciful God at work delivering you? Is that time right now?

Where is God when I am self-absorbed?

He is being merciful to me

> The Lord spoke to Jonah a second time: "Get up and go …"
> (Jonah 3:1–2)

While others gave up on me long ago, God still sees something in me worth salvaging. When I am only outwardly obeying Him from a heart that is still self serving, God is still willing for me to be His servant. He shows His mercy on me by giving me yet another chance to obey Him from a heart full of His compassion for other people.

God's patient mercy is extraordinary. He has every reason to forget about Jonah and choose someone else. He could just let Jonah keep running away, but He intervenes. He could just let Jonah drown when he is thrown overboard, but He has mercy once again. While Jonah has no compassion for Nineveh, God could bring judgment on Jonah, but instead He patiently reasons with the obstinate prophet.

Mercy is not getting what I deserve. I deserve punishment because I have sinned, yet instead of punishment, what does God give me? Another chance! Mercy me! He has so much mercy on me!

You may feel ashamed and disqualified because of past mistakes. However, the privilege of serving God is not something that can be earned. No one is qualified to serve Him. You can serve Him because He gives you His undeserved favor. Mercy and grace go hand in hand. Mercy is not getting what you deserve; grace is getting what you do not deserve.

A man in India carried two pots on opposite ends of a pole. One pot was perfect. It was always full after the man walked from the stream to his house. The other pot was cracked and only half full of water when it arrived.

While the perfect pot was very proud of its accomplishments, the cracked pot was miserable because it had accomplished only half of what was intended. One day at the stream, the unhappy pot spoke to its master.

"I want to apologize to you. I am ashamed because I leak all the way back to your house. You are not getting full value from me."

The master had compassion on the pot and said, "Have you noticed all the beautiful wildflowers on the trail back to the house? They grow only on your side of the path. Without you being the way you are, I would not have the beauty of those flowers leading to my house."

Thank you, God, for having mercy on me. Thank you for looking at me, and while overlooking my imperfections, seeing a useful vessel.

Where is God when I am self-absorbed?

He is pulling up my root of bitterness

> The Lord replied, "Is it right for you to be angry?" (Jonah 4:4)

If you are not careful, the longer your life story becomes, the more you decide that too many people have hurt you. You will have become not just older, but bitterer and less trusting. You may even start keeping a list of those who have wronged you.

Perhaps God will be on that list. When you are self-absorbed, you become bitter at others and at God. Just as He did with Jonah, God is trying to partner with you in dealing with your bitterness.

Korean pastor Paul Cho pastors the largest church in the world. As the Yoido Full Gospel Church became international, Paul prayed, "Lord, I will go anywhere you want me to go. Just don't send me to Japan."

For Paul Cho, the Japanese people were his Ninevites. The Japanese are unforgivable enemies of his own people. During World War II, the Japanese occupied Korea and China and committed many atrocities. There are still many gaping wounds and it's still a cause for ongoing bitterness.

Like many Koreans, Paul had a root of bitterness toward the Japanese people, but God already had a plan to get rid of Paul's bitterness by calling Paul to go on a mission trip to Japan. While there, Paul had the opportunity to speak to a group of Japanese pastors. He rose to speak to them, and the first words that came out of his mouth were a bit too truthful.

"I hate you. I *hate* you!"

The depth of his bitterness caused him to crumble at the podium and weep. That's all he could do.

Stunned, Japanese pastors watched this hurting Korean man in front of them. Slowly they came to Paul, knelt at his feet, and said, "Please forgive us." That day, a new spirit was born in Paul. His bitterness toward the Japanese people was removed, as God gave him a heart of love for his enemies.[51]

When you decide to *try* being sovereign, you become frustrated with God for actually *being* sovereign. Now you've taken on the Jonah mindset and have become delusional about being in control. Your main problem is that God is not cooperating with your delusion. Bitterness makes your whole life miserable.

The poisonous root of bitterness goes very deep and wide in the heart. Are you bitter about how people have treated you unfairly? God should have come to your aide and struck your enemy, yet He hasn't done anything to get even with them. In fact, He has some crazy notion about showing mercy to your enemies. Does that make you bitter toward Him?

God works to bring you to a point of desperation, where you are forced to let Him reach deep down and pull out the root of bitterness.

Do you have any root of bitterness toward anyone? With God's strength, you are empowered to love your enemies as God loves them. However, you must first examine yourself to see if there are people you do not like or who have hurt you. Do you desire to see them in pain?

Lord, you have pity even on awful, brutal people. I am so different from You. Thank you for loving me despite me. Help me to see others through Your eyes.

Where is God when I am self-absorbed?

He is revealing His compassion to me

> Should I not have compassion …? (Jonah 4:11 NASV)

According to Jonah 4:2, God is
- gracious,
- compassionate,
- slow to get angry,
- filled with unfailing love,
- not eager to destroy people, and
- desiring all people to come to Him.

Realize this: compassion requires action. In order to be compassionate, we need to show it, not just feel it. We are quick to show compassion to our friends, but how open are we to being compassionate to people we don't like?

God called Jonah to reach out beyond his comfort zone to speak the message of God to the enemies of God's people. You live in a day where your city is full of perpetrators of rampant crime. The world is full of ruthless dictators, child abusers, porn pushers, serial killers, car bombers, and self-absorbed people. Do you tend to think these people are beyond hope? Is your human desire for them to get what they deserve?

Since God has given you so many chances to try again, shouldn't you be willing to give other people another chance? Who is it that has frustrated you or made you angry?

How does the story end?

The book of Jonah ends with a question:

> Nineveh has ... people living in spiritual darkness ... Shouldn't I feel sorry...? (Jonah 4:11)

On this, the final test of his life, how does Jonah answer the one and only question on the exam? We don't know. Did he pass or fail in overcoming self-absorption? We simply don't know. Despite our demand for closure, the Jonah story ends without telling us how Jonah responds.

Does he see his own self-absorption and write what we now call the book of Jonah so that through his example we could overcome self-centered living? It could be.

Or does Jonah continue stubbornly refusing to let God change his heart? It could be. We are left without an ending.

The Jonah story doesn't end. At its end, the Jonah drama we've been watching together makes us stay tuned for an ending that's supposedly coming later. Why doesn't the story end?

It's not just a story about Jonah; otherwise the Bible would have told us how it ends. It is your story, and your life is not over yet. Your own ministry portrait is unfinished. What you will become is yet to be determined. The book of Jonah is a challenge for your life. It is kind of like stories that the ending changes based on which page you turn to.

Through Jonah you can realize a great deal about yourself. What your life will look like at the end will be determined by how you respond to the work of God in your times of self-absorption.

God, I want to break free from me. Help me give and receive compassion in my Nineveh. God, you are patiently in my face about my lack of compassion and my self-centered values. Your passion is for all people to know You. Lord, give me your passion for all kinds of people.

The rest of your story is still unwritten. If all the world's a stage, like Shakespeare said, what will you do on the stage where God has placed you?

This book would not be complete without examining two more things: a look at what the New Testament says about Jonah, and a look at what Jesus has to say about self. In the final two chapters, you will see the church and yourself more clearly than you ever have before.

When the Church Becomes Self-Absorbed

THERE ONCE WAS A DANGEROUS seacoast known for shipwrecks. Men decided to build a rescue station there. At first, it was just a hut with one small boat outside. The devoted members kept a constant watch over the turbulent sea. With no thought for themselves, they went out day and night searching for those in danger. Through this brave band of men, many lives were saved. The lifesaving station soon became a famous place.

Some of those who had been saved by the people at the station gave their time and money to support its work. Together, they bought new boats, trained rotating crews, and watched with pride as the little station began to grow.

However, some of the members complained about how small the hut was and how unattractive it had become. So all the emergency cots were replaced with feather beds. The hut was torn down to make room for all the extra rescue equipment that had been purchased.

Soon, many people began to gather at the new station, so they added on a clubhouse wing. The place was becoming a popular gathering spot for public events. Saving the lives of drowning people became the "rich heritage" of the place, yet that was no longer its primary purpose.

Of course, the life-saving motif was still very prominent in the clubhouse decorations. A full-size lifeboat was hung from the rafters in the clubhouse entryway. Since the members were more interested in socializing than roughing the sea, they hired professional lifeboat crews to do all the work.

One day a large ship wrecked off the coast. The boat crews brought in loads of half-drowned and desperate people. Some of them were also sick. Others had a bad smell. Many of the rescued were of a different ethnicity than most club members. The beautiful new clubhouse had become messy and cluttered because of "those people."

A special committee was quickly formed, and they decided to install makeshift showers and shelters outside the clubhouse so the victims could be cleaned up before coming inside.

There were strong words spoken among the members of the club. The club found that it was divided. The largest group wanted to stop all unpleasant activity and involvement related to nasty shipwrecks.

"It's a hindrance to our social lives. It opens the door to people who are not our kind," some said.

Though there was a small group who insisted the place stick to its original purpose, they were voted down and told to begin a rescue station somewhere down the coast. That is what they did.

As the years rolled on, the new station went through the same changes, evolving into just another club. Yet another lifesaving station opened even farther down the coast. If you visit that coast today, they say you will find many impressive, exclusive clubs along the shoreline. Each of them are owned and operated by smooth professionals who have lost any involvement in saving lives.

Shipwrecks are still happening in those waters, but now most victims are lost at sea. Every day they perish, and so few seem to care—so very few.[52]

Is the church self-absorbed?

Is the church asleep in a storm?

> A violent storm ... threatened to send them to the bottom ... And all this time Jonah was sound asleep down in the hold. (Jonah 1:4–5)

God is calling us to go out into the storm and find shipwreck survivors. But today's church seems it would rather stay warm and cozy in a holy huddle, praising God for shelter from the storm.

Yes, the church sends a few people up to the deck every once in a while to check on the conditions in the real world. They come back to the hull and report that everything out there is a big storm. The economy is in trouble, the community is in transition, the moral fiber of society is weakened, global warming is imminent, blah, blah, blah. The church people concur that the world is in a big mess, but the sweet fellowship within the safety of the church walls is wonderful. We think it's best to stay below deck where we can ignore the storm.

The church that is in hiding from the world does an awesome job of rationalizing. "Let's just make the church a place where a Christian family's total needs—social, recreational, educational, and spiritual—can be met.

No longer do we choose to hang out in public places, send our kids to public school, or make friends with our neighbors. All of that is taken care of by our wonderful church."

While there is some value in church recreation, church fellowship, and private Christian schools, have we allowed these fringe benefits to become more important than reaching our communities with God's love?

Has the church forgotten her original purpose of rescuing people from the storm? Has she become a club for people enjoying peace from the storm outside? Are we saved, satisfied, and sleeping? What will it take for the church to wake up, get up, and go rescue those who are drowning in the storm?

Is the church of today self-absorbed?

Is the church preoccupied with comfort?

> Then Jonah went out to the east side of the city and made a shelter ... a leafy plant ... spread its broad leaves over Jonah's head ... and Jonah was very grateful. (Jonah 4:5–6)

Jonah is far more concerned about creating a comfortable structure for himself than he is concerned about the spiritual condition of the people of Nineveh.

I had the joy of spending many years serving God among people who do not think of the church as a building. Many of my friends in Asia have never even seen a physical structure dedicated solely to the purpose of worship. When they hear the word church, they don't think of a building.

I am talking about churches who gather in factories, in places of business, in restaurants, and in homes. They've never been to church; they are the church. They are the living, walking body of Christ doing His will and His work in the world today. As they do so, they invest themselves in people far more than they do in a physical structure used a few hours a week.

In these simple churches, the focus is on Jesus Christ changing the lives of people. Very little if any money or time is spent on facilities. Those things are so boring compared to Jesus. Abundant life flows from these gatherings of the church.

What percentage of your church's budget is spent on building debt and maintenance? Last year, if your church's total income was divided by the number of people led to Christ, how much money did it take to lead one person to Christ? In an informal study of three typical American churches, I discovered that it took an average of $300,000 to lead one person to Jesus. In contrast, the typical house church on mission with God might only spend ten dollars in the process of leading one person to Christ.

While the church's primary purpose is to lift up Jesus to those who need Him, in some cases, churches are spending more than 95 percent of their income on building debt, salaries, and other self-servicing expenses. Church members seldom complain, since they enjoy the comfort of the nice structure and the pampering by the staff. Is the money churches are spending helping save the lost? Or is money merely being used for creature comforts?

Jonah sat in the shade of his self-made shelter to see what would happen to the city. With our comfortable church buildings, we take pride in what we've built and we assume the role of spectator. We comfortably watch the world go by from within the security of our walls without getting involved with the challenges of the world around us. It's like staying in a five-star hotel in an impoverished third-world country. We sip our coffee, peek out the window, and chat about the despicable conditions we see outside. We are quick to chastise but slow to go out and facilitate change. What is the church doing to change the world outside her walls?

Is the church of today self-absorbed?

Is the church slow to accept people who are "different"?

> So he complained to the Lord ... "I knew how easily you could cancel your plans for destroying these people. Just kill me now, Lord!" (Jonah 4:2–3)

Jonah complained that God's sphere of concern extended out to all people. He simply did not want God caring about *those* people. They were enemies of people like Jonah. Jonah wanted God to destroy them.

Were the church of today to be asked by God to do what was required of Jonah, we might also complain with the degree of drama produced by Jonah.

Do what? Go and care about the people living on the other side of the railroad tracks? God, you've got to be kidding! They don't deserve grace. They worked themselves into a mess; they deserve to be in poverty.

You want me to go where? Leave my spacious home and caring friends and go walk in the dangerous part of town among hateful heathens who can't even speak normal English? God, do you think I was born yesterday?

Tell them to come to our *worship? Let our comfortable church get infested with outsiders coming among us with their own strange ideas of how to worship God? Good Lord! Whose church is this, anyway?*

When core leaders of an all-white congregation were asked about the ethnic makeup of the church in comparison to the ethnic diversity in the local community, the response was appalling.

"We don't mind if they join our church, as long as they accept our values. If they want to join us, they can become like us. We wouldn't go into their places and try to change them. They shouldn't come here and expect us to change."

We may camouflage our prejudice a bit better than Jonah did. We may put our ethnic bias into words that appeal to human reason, but the bottom line is we want to worship with people who look like us, live like us, and think like us. What will we do when we get to heaven and there are people from every tribe and tongue on the planet?

The question "Whose church is it, anyway?" is extremely relevant. If it is our gathering, we can turn it into whatever kind of club we want. If it belongs to Jesus as His body, then we must be His hands reaching out to all kinds of people. We must have his heart of compassion for all people.

It is a fallacy to think that the people of our own version of Christianity have the purest values in comparison to others. Could we, if we would only be willing to learn from those who are different from us, admit that we have room for improvement? Do we really expect others to do all the changing, while we have no need for change? Are we hoping to make people into our own image while we ourselves are far from being like God? The problem is pride. We are too prideful to accept anything other than what comes from us. Could it also be fear? Are we afraid that we may be wrong?

Think of the people near the place where you worship who seem to be far from God. These people are so different from people like you in your church. Right now, your church may not be actively reaching out to them, and maybe you don't want to. What attitude changes are necessary for your church to have God's compassion for these people?

What should your church do to reach out to them?

Is the church more like a social club or a lifesaving station? Is the church today self-absorbed?

Does the church seek the spectacular?

If Jesus were to have a conversation with the leaders of His body today, what would He have to say? Let's take a look at an actual conversation between Jesus and the leaders of God's people. In this discussion, Jesus uses Jonah and the people of Nineveh as an object lesson.

> One day some teachers of religious law and Pharisees came to Jesus and said, "Teacher, we want you to show us a miraculous sign to prove that you are from God." (Matthew 12:38)

In this passage we have the Pharisees, a group of leaders from the congregation. They come to Jesus asking for Him to do something that will cause the congregation to stand at attention and say, "Wow!"

Jesus, How about a fantastic healing, or maybe raising someone from the dead to prove yourself? That would get people's attention!

Church leaders today often pray asking the Lord to work in spectacular ways. Though the prayer itself may not be in error, the motivation may be wrong. The intent of the prayer may not be to give God glory but to satisfy man's craving for a spectacular show.

Is the church just too busy creating a fabulous image? We think that God has an image problem lately, so we pray for God to work wonders for the church image to improve. We think that if God did a miracle in our church, our community would respect us more. We fail to see how God is at work, and think He is making us look bad because He isn't moving in a turning-water-into-wine way. Jonah thought God was making him look bad too.

We want people to know that God may be dead at other churches, but at *our* church He is alive and mightily at work. *Our* church knows just how to put God's spectacular works in the spotlight. Now, if God would just show up at our church and really do something!

Churches touting spectacular works of God often attract people who serve God only to get something sensational from Him. It's all about what God can do for us, not what we can do for Him.

God, give me a light streaming from heaven at midnight tonight! Then I'll know You love me and will provide a way for me!

Churches that tantalize people with spectacular works must keep increasing the dose of marvel to satisfy sensation seekers. It's like drugs.

Once you start a reliance on drugs, you will have to keep taking more and more to achieve the same effect.

Gone is the maturing process of seeing God's goodness even in the middle of everyday suffering and tedium. How does God feel about the human desire for the miraculous and the instant?

> But Jesus replied, "Only an evil and faithless generation would ask me for a miraculous sign; but the only sign I will give them is the sign of the prophet Jonah." (Matthew 12:39)

God sees us as evil when we will not believe unless God proves Himself through supernatural displays of power. Faith believes without proof. God is pleased with the people of Nineveh because they simply hear the word and believe, without any other proof given.

When Jesus was in the wilderness, the devil wanted Jesus to show His divine nature by performing miracles on demand. Jesus told the devil it is wrong to test the Lord and ask for a sign.

Do our churches ask for a sign from God? Do our churches overburden themselves with financial debt while expecting God to perform a financial miracle? Do our churches program themselves with a myriad of endless meetings and activities and expect God to show up at all of them with a magic wand in His hand? Do we focus on being fabulous, as if the greatness of our events will captivate people? Do our churches use God as a means to their own ends?

"The world can entertain more successfully than we can. But we have something far better, far richer, and far deeper to offer. We can offer life. And life is found nowhere else but in the Son of Man who came to serve,"[53] Wes Roberts and Glenn Marshall wrote in their book *Reclaiming God's Original Intent for the Church*.

If it's not programs, buildings, and attendance records that the church should focus on, what is it?

> "For as Jonah was in the belly of the great fish for three days and three nights, so I, the son of man, will be in the heart of the earth for three days and three nights." (Matthew 12:40)

Jesus clearly challenges His people to get back to the Gospel message: His death and resurrection. Though marketing the church may have some limited value, and though creating programs that meet the needs of people in the community may have some legitimacy, everything the church does or is considering doing should be prayerfully and ruthlessly evaluated in light of whether or not it lifts up the crucified and resurrected Jesus as Lord.

Churches today often seek some powerful confirmation of God's existence and His love. What greater sign is there than the death and resurrection of Jesus?

Is the church self-absorbed?

Will the church fall under God's judgment?

> "The people of Nineveh will rise up against this generation on judgment day and condemn it, because they repented at the preaching of Jonah." (Matthew 12:41)

What a surprising role reversal: Jesus says people who appear to be far from the things of God will on judgment day evaluate those who appear to be very religious. God is full of surprises! He does not see people or situations as we do.

The leaders of the religious institution considered the people of Nineveh beyond hope. However, when they repented, God gave them judges' seats in heaven. They will judge those who judged them. Let that be a warning. Those whom you judge may have the opportunity to judge you.

God does not evaluate man's spirituality based on pious-sounding prayers, length of time attending church, sacrifices made before men in beautiful temples, candles lit at the altar, religious robes worn, beautiful chants and confessions recited, or fervor in singing contemporary Christian karaoke on the worship screen.

God would rather have a group of murderers coming to Him with broken, repentant hearts than a group of respectable citizens who act religious on Sunday yet live for themselves the rest of the week. In the books of Matthew, Mark, Luke, and John, Jesus speaks out more against hypocrites of the religious establishment than He does against thieves and prostitutes.

When Christianity becomes more concerned with image, budgets, buildings, and numbers and refuses to repent of self-absorption, we can be certain that at judgment day there will be people like the repentant terrorists of Nineveh whom God will use to condemn the church for being fake. Could it be that even now judgment is on the institutionalized church of America?

Would God destroy what He has built? Though on the individual level God is patient with Jonah, on the corporate level it's a different matter. When the religious institution, which God started, becomes self-absorbed, God stands ready to destroy His own institution.

God created people for relationship with Him, yet they became self-absorbed. God instituted the Ten Commandments to help people know the Lord. The law failed to bring people back to God.

God instituted a system of sacrificing animals as a way to be rid of self-absorption, but that system also failed because people were not giving their hearts to God.

In each case, when an institution no longer fulfilled God's purpose of bringing people back into relationship with the Creator, God sidestepped the institution He created to accomplish His purpose from another angle.

Finally, God gave the greatest sacrifice. While we were self-absorbed, He gave His only Son to die in our place. God has created the relatively new institution we call the church, the body of Christ.

Will the church learn from her history?

The church started out as a highly relational, flexible, and rather spontaneous gathering of people all bringing something to the potluck table of worship. There was high accountability because followers of Jesus shared their lives completely. Within the first three hundred years of the church's life, as wildfire church planting movements occurred, no less than 10 percent of the known world had decided to follow Jesus.

Then something happened. In 313 A.D., the ruler Constantine declared that Christianity would be the official religion of the land. Huge sanctuaries were built, and all things holy went into the hands of paid professionals.

The lifesaving work of the church slowly became a memory as the church became more like a club of people who enjoyed being with people like themselves. Though outsiders came needing to be rescued, the church preferred to hide behind stained glass. The church lost her original purpose and became a rigid institution.

Will the church go the way of other institutions of the past and fail to fulfill her purpose?

When the church is self-absorbed and refusing to repent, God is preparing unexpected people to pronounce coming judgment. Though God is extremely patient with individuals like Jonah who are self-absorbed, self-absorbed churches are an abomination to the God who so loved the world that He gave His only Son so that all people would have a chance at eternal life.

If the church is self-absorbed, let us repent and return to the outward focus of reaching our Nineveh. Let us do so before certain judgment comes. If we do not, be certain that God will raise up a replacement for church-ianity as we practice it today.

Is there any future for the church?

To be certain, God is in control and will do whatever it takes to draw all people to Him. In places of the world where persecution does not allow Christianity to become a rigid, formal institution, simple churches based on the New Testament model are full of life and are multiplying. Churches under persecution often grow very fast, while churches enjoying prosperity more easily fall into spiritual stagnation.

Even in the United States, it is refreshing to see emerging organic, spontaneous groups of Jesus lovers who are outwardly focused but inwardly transparent in doing life together, genuinely worshiping God and giving self away for the sake of all kinds of people. These fellowships care much more about authentic life transformation than they do about institutional maintenance through budgets, buildings, programs, and attendance records.

Let us not be so focused on patching cracks in the old wine skins of our institution that we fail to accept and rejoice in the new wineskins God is filling with new wine.

God is at work challenging our local church to rise above self-serving attitudes. Church seems to have become optional for many people. And why not? If church is a group of people focusing on themselves and their individual needs, who needs it?

God doesn't need a self-absorbed church, and neither do those looking to the church to give them life's bigger picture. When the church is self-absorbed, God calls churches to get up and go. Go beyond self-serving. Go to those in the city who are different from those inside the church walls. Go to those who might be threatening. Go love the enemy.

> "And now someone greater than Jonah is here—and you refuse to repent." (Matthew 12:41)

Someone greater than Jonah is here. The future of the church is in Jesus' hands. Were it in the hands of you and me, it might as well be in Jonah's hands.

- Jonah was a mere man. Jesus is God in human flesh.
- Jonah obeyed part-time from a divided heart. Jesus obeyed from a fully surrendered heart.
- Jonah only took a crazy three-day ride in a whale. Jesus actually died, was buried, and rose again.
- Jonah wanted people to die. Jesus gave life to people.
- Jonah reluctantly went to one city. Jesus ministered everywhere He went.
- Jonah's message was judgment. Jesus' message is grace. [54]

The church has a future only to the degree she becomes less like Jonah and more like Jesus. The church must fulfill her purpose in bringing all kinds of people to a place of repentance in Jesus. He alone is sufficient evidence to believe in God. Jesus will build His church as we put Him in the spotlight. He radically changes people, and changed people change churches.

Jesus expected repentance but did not find it among the outwardly religious. Oh, they were good religious, hard-working citizens, but Jesus saw through their fake front. They were far more concerned about maintaining their religious institutions than they were about genuinely following Jesus. They were merely seeking God to do something sensational so that their religious institutions would make them look good. Will we be like them, or will we repent?

Will we repent of the pride of boasting in the attendance and glory of "our church"? Will we repent of making the church into a holy huddle instead of a lifesaving station? Will we repent of focusing on our comfortable church building instead of focusing on people who need the Lord?

Breaking Free... From Me

    The church must go back to the basics of bringing people to repentance in Jesus Christ. When it comes to knowing the reality of God, what more proof does a person need than Jesus? Does a person look at light and say, "Prove to me that this is light?" There is no greater proof than the light itself. Jesus is His own evidence. He is the future of His church.

    In Him there is so much more to life than me.

So Long Self!

We have this human dilemma: what to do with self. It's not easy being me. You should try it sometime! As I think about Jonah, I look into my own heart and don't always like what I see.

It's strange, but even though there is only one of me, I can't always agree with myself. There seem to be a million roads in front of me, each calling out for me to choose only one. Life is so confusing!

I want to care about others, but I find myself dominating conversations, complaining, gossiping, being inflexible, and daydreaming about me. OK, I confess. I love others for what I get in return. My number one operating principle in life seems to be, "What's in it for me?" I get so tired of me, though, I go out looking for some other operating principle. Guess I still haven't fully bought into a life principle that makes me live for something or Someone other than merely … me. Is there more to life than just me? Please tell me there is.

There seems to be so much holding me back from being the me I want to be. When it comes to living, I'm just not always in the zone. How can I ever get there?

Maybe your struggle is similar to mine. You've tried self-help books and seminars. You've taken psychology classes about self-actualization. Thinking what you needed was more self love, you indulged in whatever your heart desired, but none of these things resulted in you being more fully alive in the end. In fact, they left you feeling even more confused.

At times maybe you've thought that what you needed was a special person in your life. Although you greatly value and desire a long-term relationship, you instead fall into repeated feel-good, spur-of-the-moment flings. That has led to self-inflictions of pain for which you're now kicking yourself.

Maybe you look for the real you in your work identity. People always ask what kind of work you do. Maybe if you had a snazzier answer to that question, you would feel better about who you are. So you push yourself as a professional, thinking vocational achievement could bring you a sense of self. At the end of the day, all you find is that you are a tired workaholic less like the you whom you want to be.

How can you discover the real you and truly begin to live? Though there seems to be a million roads before you, in fact there are only two. One

Breaking Free... From Me

has a grand sign with flashing neon lights that read "Find Self Boulevard." The other has a two-thousand-year-old faded sign that says "Lose Self Lane." You cannot travel both. If you go by one, you lose the other.

We've seen Jonah's take on self. He bought into the idea that life was all about getting things his own way, and the result was misery. It's time we look at Jesus' take on self. The way to become the real you that the Creator intended you to be is by giving up your goal of finding yourself. Jesus made the path extremely clear; the Jesus life brings lasting joy.

> If you cling to your life, you will lose it; but if you give it up for me, you will find it. (Matthew 10:39)

Is It Really Possible to De-Self? How?

Yes, it certainly is possible to be fully alive and live in the zone. Though so many people have missed out on true living, millions of people over the last two thousand years have discovered the secret. Here it is in a nutshell: *You must let Jesus transform you into a self-less person.*

This is not just psycho-babble. Jesus actually is able to save us from the miserable existence of life lived for self.

When you stop clinging to life your way and give it all up for life Jesus' way, you will be surprised to find real life.

This is so radical. It requires a total restructuring of a self-centered lifestyle. It's just too big to swallow. Let's cut Jesus' path to selflessness up into five bite-size pieces so we don't gag on it. Here's the first one.

Stop Clinging to Slippery, Selfish Stuff

> If you cling to your life … (Matthew 10:39)

In life, just as in laundry, clinging is generally not a desirable thing. Jesus warns you about trying to cling to your life. He wants you to live cling free. What does He mean? What does clinging to life look like?

It involves seeking your own comfort, security, fulfillment, ambition, and safety. If you cling to a thing, God may have to force open your fingers and release it from your grip.

The English translation of the Bible does not quite capture the essence of Jesus' words. Jesus speaks in concepts not often used in our language. He speaks of life as "breath." He speaks of the person who desires to hold on to his own breath. Let's give that a try. Cup your hands. Blow into them. Now grab that breath and hold on to it. What happens? The air escapes! Even if some of the air doesn't escape, the tighter you grasp it, the more stale and useless your own breath becomes.

When you try to cling to all things yours, you are holding on to very slippery, useless stuff. Maybe you feel that you are entitled to see your personal ambitions fulfilled, your desired career achieved, and your potential actualized. After all, these are values instilled deeply in the American dream. However, the more you push to get your way, the more you fail to grab your own breath. Even if you achieve what you set out to do, instead of satisfying you, it tricks you.

In the jungle lands, local people enjoy playing a trick on monkeys. To arouse the monkey's desire for a coconut, they will cut an opening in the coconut just large enough for the monkey's paw and then place a rock inside the coconut. The people will then put the coconut on the monkey's path through the trees.

Along comes the monkey, sees there is something unusual about this coconut, and determines he must have the treasure inside for himself. Reaching in to pull it out, he discovers that with the rock inside his paw, it is too big to come out. He has become trapped by what he thought was a treasure. Some monkeys have been known to so stubbornly refuse letting go of their treasure, they spend the rest of their lives with one arm clinging to a coconut!

Stop clinging to the slippery stuff of self. Is there a coconut you are still clinging to? What is it? Hold on loosely to the things of this life. Travel lightly. What are the things that are holding you back from really living?

Quit Losing at Life

> If you cling to your life, *you will lose it.* (Matthew 10:39)

Breaking Free... From Me

What is the goal of your life? Write your life goal in one simple phrase inside the box below.

```
┌─────────────────────────────────────────────────────────────┐
│                                                             │
│                                                             │
│                                                             │
│                                                             │
└─────────────────────────────────────────────────────────────┘
```

When your goal is self, the more you attain, the more meaningless it all becomes and you begin to self-destruct. In the original wording of the text, Jesus literally said, "The one who desires above all to keep his own breath *will be utterly destroyed.*"

I was clinging to all kinds of coconuts without even knowing it. As a missionary, I had assumed my career choice made me automatically selfless. However, one day I found myself suddenly in forced separation from all things mine.

In many countries, creative access is required to be able to share the gospel. In one such country where we lived, a security crisis dictated that I must go away by myself. The forced separation lasted three months. Gone from me was my family, my work, my home, my schedule, my life breath. Though I had prided myself on the number of lives changed and the number of new churches started through our work, I now realized that even those things were done, at least in part, toward the selfish end of receiving praise from others.

While in exile, I slowly began to see that clinging tightly to my own life had made me a loser. Though I professed to be Christ-centered, in actuality my operating life principle was doing what seemed best for self. Suddenly, I found it all slipping away. Desiring to hold on tight to all things dear to me had caused, when I had to give them all up, a severe down swing in my emotions. It was then, at rock bottom, that I gave it all up for life Jesus' way and quit losing at life. In brokenness before my Creator, full surrender of self was my only choice.

How does clinging to things make me a loser at life? It's like a young lady walking across a narrow mountain pass when her feet slip out from under her. As she begins to slide down the side of the rocky mountain, she grabs on to a bush only to find it full of thorns. Refusing to let go, the thorns just dig deeper into her flesh. Were she to look ten feet below, she would see a pool of refreshing water. She could find relief by plunging into that pool if she would only let go. However, she would rather just keep clinging and feeling like such a loser.

My clinging shows that I am afraid of losing things. Clinging is a fear-based attempt at loss prevention. Clinging prevents new things from being able to enter my life. I can become so fearful of losing things or people that I cannot enjoy having them. Clinging makes me a loser because it makes me stagnant, self-centered, and fearful. When I cling to all things self, I sometimes sacrifice integrity to get what I want, and that makes me a loser as well.

If you hold on tightly to life as you want it to be, you become a loser. Life is not meant to be unchanging. God wants you to be a work in progress. Quit trying to hold on to situations, people, and places you cannot possibly keep.

If you seek safety, ease, comfort, security, and the fulfillment of personal ambition, you may get them all, but you may find no satisfaction. If you hoard life, you will not find real life. You will only become the biggest loser, forfeiting all that makes life valuable.

If you hoard money, it can be lost in an economic downturn. If you hoard health, you could become a hypochondriac. If life is clutched, it is lost. Living for self makes you a loser. You were not made for self, but for God and others.

Self-centered living makes you into the biggest loser. What are you losing by centering life on self?

Say "So Long" to Self

> If you cling to your life, you will lose it; *but if you give it up* for me, you will find it. (Matthew 10:39)

Bobby was a terrier belonging to John Gray of Edinburgh, Scotland. One day the dog's master died. Bobby followed the funeral procession of his master all the way to the cemetery. After the funeral was over, he stayed at the grave even after everyone else left.

Bobby remained at his master's gravesite until he died fourteen years later. The people of Edinburgh were touched by the dog's loyalty to his master. The people not only went to the cemetery to feed him, but after the dog's death, they put up a statue of him. Bobby gave up his life, yet his selfless spirit lives on, inspiring people to give themselves away.

Are you giving yourself fully to God and others? What will be the one thing remembered about you when you leave this world?

Instead of living for self, give yourself away to God, family, friends, neighbors, and even your enemies. The real rule of life is not, "He who dies with the most toys wins." It is instead, "He who dies the biggest giver wins." Quit asking, "What's in it for me?" Instead ask, "How can I give myself away?"

Remember, your life will become richer in proportion to how much you spend of yourself on God and others. A life totally spent serving God and others is a life well lived.

Die to self. So long, self. Goodbye,

- Self-asserting,
- Self-will,
- Self-confidence,
- Self-consciousness,
- Self-defending,
- Self-destruction,
- Self-exalting,
- Self-helping,
- Self-indulgence,
- Self-loving,
- Self-pleasing,
- Self-seeking,
- Self-righteousness, and
- Self-will.

For Christ's Sake, Give it Up

Though my world is wrapped around little ol' me, the world of Christ is the world I now enter into. It is radically different from where I have been. How refreshing! His world is

- Self-abandoning,
- Self-abasing,
- Self-conquering,
- Self-consecrating,
- Self-controlled,

- Self-denying,
- Self-disciplined,
- Self-discovering,
- Self-examining,
- Self-giving,
- Self-knowing,
- Self-mastering,
- Self-sacrificing, and
- Self-surrendering.

> If you cling to your life, you will lose it; but if you give it up *for me*, you will find it. (Matthew 10:39)

A Web search for the term "selfless living" reveals no less than 1,140,000 sites available for your assistance. What a confusing assortment of techniques, all supposedly helping a person to shed their own skin. Philosophies abound on how to get rid of self. Many, if not most, of these Web sites teach New Age, Hindu, and Buddhist practices, which are gaining popularity among young people of America today.

Before we bash this wave of seemingly untraditional teaching coming into America, we must realize that young people of America are crying out for answers to the question, "Is there more to life than me?"

The question is extremely valid and must not be criticized. Neither should the search for answers to the question. Could part of the problem be that Jesus Christ, as presented by the institutionalized church of today, has left young people yawning with boredom? Has Christianity become a me-centered religion?

To young people, churches often appear to be so self-serving they respond by saying, "If the church is all about serving itself, give me something else. If Jesus is all about me, then I will look elsewhere for life's bigger picture."

It's time to take a fresh look at Jesus. [55] Radical and risky are the demands Christ places on us. He demands that His followers go all the way with Him to a selfless death. Jesus gives a big enough challenge to attract even the most risk-loving young person on the face of the planet. I dare you to get in on the holy rush of adrenaline that comes from recklessly and radically following the dangerous person of Jesus the Christ.

Jesus says that the one who loses his life for His sake will find the real joy of true life. Consider the context in which He shared this concept. The church of Christ was born in an environment hostile to believers in Jesus. Christians were outlawed, persecuted, hunted down, covered in tar, and lit as human streetlamps around the city of Rome. It was a crime to follow Jesus. Everyone was to declare Caesar as lord. Most Christians, however, refused and boldly confessed that Jesus was Lord.

Such radical obedience is what brings adventurous life to believers and vitality to the church. During its first few decades, when following Jesus meant risking loss of life, the church was busting out of the seams with such genuineness and excitement that the number of Christ followers grew at an average of 40 percent per decade.[56]

Such growth did not come about through buildings, budgets, bigger church parking lots, and slick advertising. Those who were giving up their lives for the sake of Christ were sharing life on life in house churches and finding true, authentic life at its best. Those looking on became desperate to get in on the action.

For those early believers, the decision to follow Jesus was not a casual repeat-after-me prayer to get saved. It wasn't a decision to *get* anything! It was, rather, a decision to *lose* everything for Jesus' sake.

"When Christ calls a man, he bids him come and die."[57] Jesus calls us to die for Him. He says that we will only find real life if we are willing, for His sake, to give it all up. In Him, you find more to life than you. You find selfless living.

He calls you to be selfless when others are happy, to rejoice with those who rejoice.

He calls on you to be selfless when others are hurting, to weep with those who weep.

He calls you to be selfless when others hurt you, to bless those who trouble you.

It's amazing what people will do in attempting to purge self of self. They will crawl along a road for thousands of miles, pierce their bodies, walk on red-hot coals, do drugs, have serial lovers, or sit with their legs crossed for hours on end saying "Ommmmm."

There are many philosophies and practices that attempt to aid people in selfless living. However, self-interest is such a powerful force that these methods only provide a temporary self-deception, not a cure for the real disease: our heart's selfish nature. There is only one way that actually changes the nature of the human heart.

Only Jesus has the power to turn self-centered you into someone who lives for God and others. Let him perform surgery on your heart, cutting out your self-centeredness and putting His Spirit within you. Surgery is painful, but it leads to health and life.

*By focusing life on the person of Jesus Christ,
you can truly lose yourself in Him.*

What does self-less living for Christ's sake look like? The house churches of communist China know all about it. There, people who want to follow Jesus are often asked five questions before they can be baptized.

- Are you ready to pray in all circumstances?
- Are you ready to share the gospel in all circumstances?
- Are you ready to suffer for Christ in all circumstances?
- Are you ready to escape if the opportunity presents itself? (Matthew 10:23 teaches believers who are persecuted in one place to flee to another.)
- Are you ready to die for Christ in all circumstances?

You have never seen people more fully alive than those who are ready to die for Jesus. When they refuse to spit on the Bible, they are brutally tortured. When they refuse to renounce Christ, they are imprisoned and even killed. Through it all they are empowered and made fully alive because they have already considered themselves as dead.

Dying to self to live for Christ means giving up personal ambitions, the ease and comfort that you might have enjoyed, the career you might have achieved, the self will of doing life your way to simplify life by doing *one* thing: whatever Christ wants.

Is this your prayer? *Whatever you want in and through me Jesus, I am not my own. I am yours. I am dead to self, alive to You.*

If you are to succeed at selfless living, the only way is death of self through the transforming power of Christ.

Humble men and women do not have a *low* opinion of themselves; they have *no* opinion of themselves, because they so rarely think about themselves. The heart of humility lies in undivided attention to God, a fascination with His beauty revealed in creation, a contemplative presence to each person who speaks to us, and a "de-selfing" of our plans, projects, ambitions, and soul.[58]

Let Real Life Take You by Surprise

> If you cling to your life, you will lose it; but if you give it up for me, *you will find it.* (Matthew 10:39)

The good life is found when you quit looking for it. It's found when you are no longer preoccupied with self but instead become absorbed in the Kingdom of God and the welfare of other people. The way to be surprised by real joy, meaning, and purpose is to spend life selflessly through the power of Christ. Risk all of life by putting self into the hands of God.

Then one day you will get to heaven and see Jesus waiting for you. He will say, "Well done. You lost your life for me. Enter in to eternal joy with me!"

If any human being ever reserved the right to be self-centered, it was Jesus. He existed before we did. He made the world we live in. He needs nothing that we can give. Yet amazingly, He is so selfless that on the cross He gave His very life for the sake of self-centered people.

He is the only perfectly selfless example worthy of being followed. When you live for Him, you are surprised to find in your life zest, purpose, power, and peace. When you die to self, you become fully alive in Him.

Let the cross move you to give as He gave. Are you ready to be surprised by life? Pray this with every ounce of your being: *Jesus, give me one pure and holy passion: to live for You.*

Choose to Live Selfless in a Self-Centered Culture

I know what you are thinking. You wish you could call me and say, "Isn't there a need to keep everything in balance and not go overboard with this surrendering of self? Shouldn't I have some spirituality without getting too sold-out about it? Can't Jesus help me meet my own goals?"

Our culture says …	Our Bible says …
You are the greatest.	"Put no confidence in the flesh. (Philippians 3:3 NKJV)"
Have it your way.	"I have been crucified with Christ. (Galatians 5:19)"
Increase your influence.	"He must increase. I must decrease. (John 3:30 NKJV)"
Never be satisfied.	"I have learned how to get along happily whether I have much or little. (Philippians 4:11)"
Get yourself noticed.	"If any of you wants to be my follower, you must put aside your selfish ambition, shoulder your cross daily, and follow me. (Luke 9:23)"
Gotta keep looking out for number one [59]	"Humble yourselves under the mighty power of God. (I Peter 5:6)"

The path to solving the problem of self is the way of Christ. If you are to truly live, you must focus your full attention on Him. Though you do not know what He has planned for you, trust His goodness and surrender self in waiting for His lead. Later, you will understand why He led you as He did. Søren Kierkegaard reminds us that, "Life is lived forward but understood backward."[59]

Is that what you are ready to say? *Jesus, set me free from self-consciousness, from concern about tomorrow, from the stress of seeking the approval of others, from the pain of selfish wanting, from the depression of doing what seems best for me, so that I truly desire to find delight in life from simply and only pleasing You. For me to live is Christ. To die is gain.*

Think about a time when it was hard for you to yield your will to God's will. Why did you have difficulty?

Two friends went to an auction. The experienced friend said to the first-timer, "There are two rules. Know your upper limit price, and don't scratch your nose at the wrong time!"

We want a relationship with Jesus, but secretly we know our upper limit price. "Jesus, I'll do most anything You ask, except …" Such clinging leads to death. You are called to a life of unconditional obedience where the price is not known. Even your own breath of life should be within your upper limit. If you want to know the big picture of how life is supposed to be, you must surrender all to Jesus.

Christians in India like to tell a story about a boy who loved to play marbles. He enjoyed walking through the neighborhood looking for children to compete at marbles. One of his marbles was his very favorite: a cracked blue one that had won him many matches.

One day on the street he met a girl eating a lot of chocolates. His tummy began to rumble, and he said, "I'll give you all my marbles for the bag of chocolates."

She said, "Sounds fair to me."

So he put his hand in his pocket, felt the cracks on the blue marble, pushed it deep down into his pocket, and pulled out all the other marbles. They made the exchange. As she walked away, he said, "Did you really give me all the chocolates?"

We want it all, without having to give up everything to gain it. There's often a blue marble we are secretly unwilling to give up to the Lord. What is your blue marble?

To sacrifice this temporary lower life for the sake of Christ is to gain a permanent, higher life. If you cannot bring yourself to give up one to gain the other, you will lose both. If for the sake of Christ you let go of living for self, you will find that self is in sync with life's bigger picture, both now and for eternity.

I recently borrowed a book from my son and daughter-in-law, Joshua and Erin Nance. In the book, Erin had underlined a verse of scripture and added her own hand-written comment after the verse. The verse said, "Most people around here are looking out for themselves, with little concern for the things of Jesus. But you know yourselves that Timothy's the real thing (Philippians 2:22, The Message)." The note after the verse said, "Let Erin be the real thing."

Let *me* be the real thing. May *you* be the real thing.

Appendix A

Self Check

As your day ends, think about the things you did today. List them here. Then put a check by the things you did to pursue or satisfy your own desires. Finally, put a check by those things you did out of a genuine desire to honor and please God.

Things I did today	Done for Self	Done to Honor God

Appendix B

Urban Centers

Place Name	UN 2010 Pop	People Name	Language	Religion
Tokyo/ Yokohama, Japan	36,093,596.00	Japanese	Japanese	Other - Shinto
Mumbai (Bombay), India	20,072,421.00	Mahratta	Marathi	Hinduism
Delhi, India	17,014,579.00	Brahman	Hindi	Hinduism
Shanghai, China	15,789,336.00	Han	Chinese	Non - believers - Secularism
Kolkata, India	15,576,565.00	Kayastha	Hindi	Hinduism
Dhaka, Bangladesh	14,795,628.00	Shaikh	Bengali	Islam
Karachi, Pakistan	13,051,716.00	Rajput	Punjabi, Western	Islam
Cairo, Egypt	12,503,374.00	Arab, Egyptian	Arabic, Egyptian	Islam - Sunni

Beijing, China	11,740,911.00	Han	Chinese, Mandarin	Non-believers - Secularism
Osaka, Japan	11,337,016.00	Japanese	Japanese	Other - Shinto
Istanbul, Turkey	10,530,033.00	Turk	Turkish	Islam - Sunni
Moscow, Russia	10,495,092.00	Russian	Russian	Christianity - Orthodox
Paris, France	9,957,855.00	French	French	Christianity - Catholic
Jakarta, Indonesia	9,702,617.00	Indonesian	Indonesian	Islam - Sunni
Guangzhou, China	9,447,341.00	Han	Chinese	Non-believers - Secularism
Tehran, Iran	8,220,570.00	Irani	Farsi, Western	Islam - Shia
Shenzhen, China	8,114,156.00	Han	Chinese	Non-believers - Secularism
Chennai (Madras), India	7,558,836.00	Adi Dravida	Tamil	Hinduism
Wuhan, China	7,542,023.00	Han	Chinese, Mandarin	Non-believers - Secularism

Endnotes

1. See Luke 12:7, 24.
2. Skip Heitzig, When God Prays (Wheaton: Tyndale, 2003), p. 22.
3. Skip Heitzig, When God Prays, p. 173.
4. Brennan Manning, Ruthless Trust (New York: Harper Collins, 2002), p. 10.
5. Rudyard Kipling, Captain Courageous (Signet Classics, 1964), as quoted in Alex and Brett Harris, Do Hard Things (Colorado Springs: Multnomah, 2008), p. 132.
6. David A. Zimmerman, Deliver Us from Me-ville (Colorado Springs: David C. Cook, 2008)
7. J. Oswald Sanders, Spiritual Leadership (Chicago: Moody Press, 1994)
8. Blanchard, Ken. "Lead Like Jesus," Seminar.
9. Charles H Spurgeon, Evening by Evening: A New Edition of the Classic Devotional Based on The Holy Bible, English Standard Version. New York: Crossway Books, 2008.
10. Catherine Yack, Think Outside the Fish. (Enumclaw: Pleasant Word-A Division of WinePress, 2008).
11. In an earlier chapter, we comically pictured Jonah being spewed out of the fish to land in front of a sign that read "Nineveh City Limits." However, scholars suggest there may have been a five-hundred mile journey from the shore where Jonah was delivered to the inland city of Nineveh. If so, Jonah's obedience required him to take a very tiresome journey through the dessert, likely on a camel. After many days of travel, he would have finally arrived at the place where God wanted him. Another possibility is that the fish swam a rapid but long distance around the Mesopotamia peninsula and up the Tigris River, which flows adjacent to where archeologists have discovered the ruins of ancient Nineveh.
12. O. Palmer Robertson, Jonah: A Study in Compassion, p. 50.

13. The old hymn "Leaning on the Everlasting Arms" proclaims that we are "safe and secure from all alarms"; however, in scripture the people of God were often involved in high-risk activities of faith. Baptist Hymnal 2008 (Nashville, Lifeway Worship), page 453.
14. Erwin Raphael McManus, The Barbarian Way. (Nashville: Thomas Nelson, 2005), p. 114.
15. Also, when Jonah later pouts about how the story ends without Nineveh being destroyed, God patiently gives Jonah yet another chance at understanding God's compassion for people.
16. Dr. Ron Jenson, Achieving Authentic Success. (Temecula, California: Future Achievement International, 2006), p. 101.
17. See Psalm 103:13, Deuteronomy 5:10, Psalm 57:10, Psalm 86:5, Exodus 3:7, Mark 1:41, Matthew 14:14, Mark 6:34, and Matthew 9:35-36.
18. Yes, not just in Heaven, but under Heaven, because He left Heaven to come to this earth to have mercy on us.
19. The Barbarian Way, 72.
20. http://www.iamsecond.com/#/seconds/Shannon_Culpepper/
21. "I Am Second" is a movement of Christ followers who meet in small groups around the United States.
22. "Keep America Christian!," sermon by Dr. Walter A. Maier, aired on the Lutheran Hour, January, 1942. Available at www.heartoftn.net
23. A few other countries may actually have a higher income per person, but in those countries the cost of living is higher.
24. See Exodus 34:27, Matthew 4:2, 6:16-18, 8:14-15, 9:14-15 for regular fasting. See also Daniel 1:12 for partial fasting, Ezra 10:6, Esther 4:16, Acts 9:9 for absolute fasting from food and water, Deuteronomy 9:9 and I Kings 19:8 for supernatural fasting, Joel 2:15 and Acts 13:2 for congregational fasting, II Chronicles 20:3 and Jonah 3 for national fasting, as well as Leviticus 16:29-31 for the annual fast. See also Judges 20:26, I Samuel 7:6, II Samuel 1:12, II Samuel 3:35, Nehemiah 9:1, Acts 9:9, 13:2, 14:23, Matthew 4, 6, 9:14-15, Isaiah 58.
25. You can also fast from things other than food.
26. He reigned from 773 to 756 B.C.

27. O.S. Hawkins, Jonah: Meeting the God of the Second Chance (Neptune, New Jersey: Loizeaux Brothers 1990), 101.
28. Offered by the Rev. Joe Wright at the new session of the Kansas Senate, January 1996.
29. For examples of corporate guilt and praying for the sins of others, see Exodus 24:9, Numbers 14:19, I Samuel 12:23, Ezra 9:6-10, Nehemiah 1:5-7, Jeremiah 14:7,20, Daniel 9:4-19, Hosea 4:6-14, Matthew 23:31-38.
30. "Provost Rice at Founders' Day calls for strength in adversity." News release, 03 Aug. 1994. Stanford University News Service. 24 Aug. 2009 <http://news-service.stanford.edu/pr/94/940308Arc4392.html>.
31. The same Hebrew word for the people "repenting" is used to describe God changing His mind about destroying their city.
32. To be clear, obeying God is better than disobeying God. I should not wait for a perfectly pure heart before I start obeying. However, my motive for obeying God is important. Do I really want to please God? God is pleased with obedience from a heart that really wants to glorify God by doing what is right.
33. Read the book of Psalms to find clear Biblical validity for sharing all your emotions with God.
34. At such a crucial, teachable time, Jonah should have lingered long among the repentant people, helping them follow God. However, self-pity has Jonah leaving them to search for God on their own. As a result, the revival at Nineveh was short lived. A few years later, the Ninevites returned to self-absorbed living and were destroyed. (See Nahum 1-3)
35. Sinclair B. Ferguson, First Presbyterian Church, Columbia, SC. Sermon preached 11 Jan. 2009.
36. George Barna, Think Like Jesus. (Nashville: Thomas Nelson, 2003), 112.
37. Paul Thompson, "Joni Eareckson Tada - Making Sense of Suffering." Christian Library. 24 Aug. 2009 <http://www.christianlibrary.org.au/schoolofsuffering/joni.html>.
38. Peter Williams, Running From God. (Surrey, UK: Day One Publications, 2003), Pg 93.

39. Brennan Manning, Ruthless Trust. (New York: Harper One, 2002), pg 64.
40. Anthony Bourdain, The Best American Travel Writing 2008. (Boston: Houghton Mifflin, 2008), 114.
41. Genesis 10:11-12
42. Dennis Lyle, You Can Run but You Cannot Hide. (Greenville: Ambassador Emerald, 2004), 100.
43. International Standard Bible Encyclopedia, (Grand Rapids, Eerdmans, 1939, Vol. III), p. 2148.
44. Nahum 1:9, 2:12-13, 3:4
45. www.imb.org/easia
46. See Appendix for a chart of the Top Twenty Unreached Cities of the World.
47. Alex and Brett Harris, Do Hard Things, (Colorado Springs: Multnomah, 2008), p. 205.
48. For a book full of ideas on reaching out to neighbors, see Field Guide to Neighborhood Outreach, Loveland, Co.: Group Publishing, 2007.
49. When I am running from God (Jonah 1), He is chasing after me. When I am running to God (Jonah 2), He is waiting to receive me with open arms. When I am running with God (Jonah 3), He uses my outward obedience despite my imperfect heart. When I am running ahead of God (Jonah 4), He is patiently correcting my perspective.
50. According to II Kings 14:25, Jonah had earlier obeyed God by announcing the restoration of the lost territory to King Jeroboam.
51. Denis Lyle, You Can Run, But You Can't Hide: The Life of Jonah. (New York: Ambassador International, 2004).
52. Marilyn Meberg, Overcoming Mistakes: A Light-hearted Look at Jonah (Light-Hearted Bible Study). (Nashville: Thomas Nelson, 2004).
53. Charles R. Swindoll, Swindoll's Ultimate Book of Illustrations & Quotes: Over 1,500 Ways to Effectively Drive Home Your Message. (Nashville: Thomas Nelson, 2003), p. 86.
54. Wes Roberts and Glenn Marshall, Reclaiming God's Original Intent for the Church. (New York: Navpress Group, 2004), p.123

55. Wiersbe, Warren W., Bible Exposition Commentary Vol. 1. (Grand Rapids: Chariot Victor, 2003), p.43
56. For a fresh look at the church, read Reclaiming God's Original Intent for the Church, by Wes Roberts and Glenn Marshall.
57. Rodney Stark, Reconstructing the Rise of Christianity: Adventures in Historical Sociology (Princeton, N.J.: Princeton University Press, 1996), p. 8.
58. Dietrich Bonhoeffer, The Cost of Discipleship (New York: Macmillan, 1977), p. 99.
59. Brennan Manning, Ruthless Trust (New York: Harper Collins, 2002), p. 120.
60. This chart is adapted from O.S. Hawkins, Culture Shock: Advice from Daniel for Addressing Today's Culture, Annuity Board, 2002, p. 112.
61. Søren Kierkegaard, Purity of Heart is to Will One Thing, (New York: Harper and Row, 1948), p. 102.

CPSIA information can be obtained
at www.ICGtesting.com
Printed in the USA
BVHW031303270919
559632BV00001B/2/P